How to NOT *Know You're Trans*

A Memoir of the Unknown Trans Person

and How A Marriage Survived and Thrives Through It

by
Bethany A. Beeler
©2019

ISBN: 9781650034263
Beautiful Buddha Books

Other works by Bethany A. Beeler

Maria (of the angels)

Mirrororrim

The Fire Golem

Yanter (coming Spring 2020)

The Smoking Inn, With A Special Welcome to Lesbians, Trans Women, and All Creatures (forthcoming)

Caerdwain (forthcoming)

The Engine of the Avenging Angels (forthcoming)

Lawrence & the League of Short-Order Cooks (forthcoming)

The Bishop Tripped (forthcoming)

The Gods of Rome (forthcoming)

Master of the Universe (forthcoming)

SEP

For more information on Bethany's paintings and novels, go to her website at http://bit.ly/bethanybeeler

Table of Contents

for Pam

my G-d, she is it!!

Once you start to speak, people will yell at you. They will interrupt you, put you down, and suggest it's personal. And the world won't end.

And the speaking will get easier and easier. And you will find you have fallen in love with your own vision, which you may never have realized you had. And you will lose some friends and lovers and realize you don't miss them. And new ones will find you and cherish you. And you will still flirt and paint your nails, dress up and party, because, as I think Emma Goldman said, "If I can't dance, I don't want to be part of your revolution."

And at last you'll know with surpassing certainty that only one thing is more frightening than speaking your truth. And that is not speaking.
—Audre Lord

When illusion spin her net
I'm never where I want to be
And liberty she pirouette
When I think that I am free
Watched by empty silhouettes
Who close their eyes but still can see
No one taught them etiquette
I will show another me
Today I don't need a replacement
I'll tell them what the smile on my face meant
My heart going boom, boom, boom
"Hey," I said, "You can keep my things, they've come to take me home."
—Peter Gabriel/"Solsbury Hill"

Foreword

This is my memoir, which means you get my side of the story. That there are perhaps a thousand other sides of the story is for multiverse dimensional theorists to debate. As my memoir, it reflects the subjective bias I bring even to my most fervently intended-to-be-objective self-analysis. Read this book, and you get me, for better/for worse.

I am aware that some of my reminiscences may be compromising for those who were involved with me in those past-events. Thus, I alter names to afford privacy.

Last, my memoir explores mature themes of human sexuality and gender identity. I do not believe there's a standard age limit for when a person is ready for such things. So, I don't label this title as containing material suitable only for those 18 and over. I know from my own experience that persons of all ages need to hear what is said in this book, if only to bring many of them hope and the revelation that they're not alone. So, if you're a parent, please read this memoir before you dismiss it as "inappropriate" for your offspring. You simply don't know till you read it. If after that, you chuck it out of a plane a continent away from your kids, that's your prerogative.

But know this. All of this happened.

And I'm alive to tell it.

Preface

The dominant-culture-accepted (*if* it's accepted) trans narrative can be summed up with "I grew up a boy/girl trapped in a girl's/boy's body."

It's a narrative you may have heard multiple times in media presentations of trans persons—painful realization at a tender age, rejection by parents, siblings, peers, religious groups, and the gender-binary-obsessed culture at large. Struggle to assert identity. Breaking free into a new life.

I don't condemn this narrative, for it's all too real and accounts for a certain population's trans and non-binary experience. What portion of the trans population identifies with this narrative? Truth to tell, we don't know because we're still learning about what it means to be trans. As with any minority group that breaches the dominant culture's fortress, it's the first stories the dominant culture finds amenable that determine the thereafter stereotyped narrative of the minority group. Only years, if not decades, later do we discover that that minority's experience is varied, nuanced, and less cookie-cutter than the stereotyped narrative indicates.

Which doesn't mean that narrative isn't authentic. Nor does it mean that the pain those persons experience and the courage they demonstrate in living to tell their stories is therefore nil because their stories are the mainstreamed trope by which the dominant culture acknowledges that minority. But it *can* mean that narrative becomes the *only* experience of the minority that the dominant culture grudgingly accepts.

In the West, it took the gay and lesbian community millennia to be seen as persons having an identity. Greco-Roman culture viewed homosexuality as merely a preference that organized Christianity declared sinful outside the bounds of monogamous cisgender heterosexual marriage. The term, "homosexuality" wasn't coined until the late 19th century, 100 years before the

Compton's Cafeteria and Stonewall riots and the Pride movement blasted off the lid pressed down by the dominant culture. It took nearly another 50 years before the U.S. Supreme Court Obergefell decision legalized same-sex marriage.

The "T" in the LGBTQIA+ alphabet had been, until recently in Western culture, literally unacknowledged, aside from the tabloid fodder of Christine Jorgensen's (1951) and Reneé Richards' (1975) transitions. Despite these comparatively high-profile trans figures, trans identity was (and, in many quarters, still is) categorized as, at best, a mental illness or a comic's punchline and, at worst, a perversion. Despite the key roles of trans persons in the Compton's Cafeteria and Stonewall riots and the Pride movement, even those in the LGB community shunned (and some still shun) trans persons—either agreeing with the notion that such was a perversion/mental illness or tamping down the trans identity as a hindrance to the popular embrace of gay and lesbian rights.

But the times they are acceleratin'. Read *Time Magazine's* May 29, 2014 "The Transgender Tipping Point" today, and it sounds archaic, given the milestone accomplishments made by the trans movement (and accompanying blowback) within the following five-plus years. Even though a majority of Americans (as of this writing) still say they've never met/encountered a trans person, upwards of 60% of Americans in a majority of demographic groups express support for the acceptance of trans persons and trans rights. 1951 to 2019 is less than 70 years.

With the acceleration of trans acceptance, trans stories call for the variety and nuance provided by something other than "I grew up a boy/girl trapped in a girl's/boy's body." Indeed, it's a matter of life and death. The unabated murders of trans persons of color show that hearing these variant voices will save lives.

Not that my story or those of trans persons of color or anyone's is more authentic or normative than other narratives. They aren't … and that's the point. We need *everyone's* story, as much as a masterwork painting needs more than one color/shade and a song needs more than one chord.

And my story is this:

- I didn't *become* a woman; I've *always* been a woman.

- I didn't need to know from an early age that I wasn't at home in my assigned-at-birth gender in order for my transition to be "authentic" (in whose esteem this authenticity should matter, I'm not sure—I'm me; if you don't like it, that's your problem).

- I never needed to know that I wanted to transition until I was ready to transition. So what if I didn't consciously know until I was 54 that I was a woman assigned a male gender at birth on the basis of the presentation of my genitalia?

- In fact, I never "transitioned," if, by that, you mean that I "changed" from being a man to being a woman at a later date in my life. As Janet Mock has noted—"I wasn't born a boy or a girl. I was born a baby."

Oh, honey, I did most certainly *transition* … from living a miserable life in which I portrayed myself as the man I thought I had to be to a reality in which I, for the first time, am joyfully able to be me.

Chapter 1

When I Happened on the Way to Being Me

In 2018, I happened on the way to being me.

I didn't merely come out MtF transgender; I discovered I was trans in the first place—as much news to me as it became to the world.

One could hope that every nanosecond anniversary we become more ourselves, but that road trip isn't an expressway progression. Some years are better than others. On December 31, 2017, to quote the movie, *Hot Fuzz*, I had "a great big bushy beard." A year later, I had breasts! Yes, *real breasts,* as I hit my true puberty.

Some years are worse than others. Those years when my body writhed in its male-assigned puberty, were the most horrific of my existence. I'd no idea what was happening. For the next 40 orbits of the sun, I lost me—the real me, disappearing in my rearview mirror. Hitching a ride in place of absent me came anxiety, depression, and OCD that, teamed with my smarts, gave me the roadmap to plot out that I was miserable but also to frustrate every effort for the next 40 years to grasp why.

In what I thought at the time was a valiant effort to keep the tires between the lines, I sped through ideologies and tribes, one after another, to find a home, or at least a way-place where I could drop the rusting, screeching, tail-lights-out trailer that was life, if only for a few seconds. Every rest stop was as unfulfilling as a kid dreaming of Disney World, only to see that Exit 123 is another Shoney's.

I swore off rest stops and found that the car breaks down if you don't gas it, change the oil, and fill the tires. So, about 15 years ago, I took antidepressants and therapy like a performance vehicle takes synthetic oil, to belay the inevitable breakdowns.

The thing is, I didn't know *why* my life was this goddamned Interstate trip. I kept running on empty, a la Jackson Browne and *Forrest Gump*. "Run, Babsie, Run!!" Except I wasn't Babsie. I wasn't even me. I'd no idea that life didn't have to be pounding asphalt, glaring headlights, and XXX stores at the seedy exits.

Then I met Bethany (aka Babsie). It was like falling in love for the first time—which I was (and still am) with myself, my *real self*. In *Little Gidding,* T.S. Eliot describes arriving "at where we started [to] know the place for the first time." I've been up and down this Interstate on countless trips, but, damn! I'm seeing Bethany billboards of me for the first time and finding I *like* Shoney's.

I enjoy coffee with Babsie. She's fun. She doesn't blow up at inconsequential shit, like the cruise control not working. Babs and I most often get the French Toast, with the fake maple syrup. We appreciate the wait staff, especially Cora, who nests a gross of pens in her bouffant but keeps smiling—not in spite of working at Shoney's but *because* she works at Shoney's.

Bethany went through my male puberty, locked in the trunk. I didn't hear her banging the hatch with the tire iron till I'd run out of gas and settled on walking the interstate, noting roadkill. Bethany didn't yell at me when I let her out of the trunk. She didn't yank out my beard or tear at my nipples demanding they become lady boobies. She hugged me. And she hasn't let go since.

It was then that I noticed I'm not on the road. I'm at home. With me.

Chapter 2

I Have Two Birthdays, Baby!

Come down off your throne and leave your body alone.
Somebody must change.
You are the reason I've been waiting so long.
Somebody holds the key.
—Steve Winwood/"Can't Find My Way Home"

Today is August 22, 2019, my 56th natal anniversary. I was born three months to the day before the assassination of JFK and the deaths of C.S. Lewis and Aldous Huxley. Despite Kennedy Camelot, Western society of the time assigned gender solely on what genitals popped out of the womb.

My natal anniversary is also the birthday of Baseball Hall of Famers Carl Yastrzemski and Paul Molitor, as well as the Catholic Feast of the Coronation of Mary, Queen of Heaven. I like the syncopation of 8/22/63. It builds on itself, promising more to come. I'm a Leo on the cusp of Virgo—a cross between a lioness and the Goddess of Love. Woo-hoo!

But I have another birthday. On March 8, 2018, my beautiful wife, Pam, crawled into bed to spoon with a very-asleep me, and whispered, "Be who you're supposed to be."

I stirred. "Izzat you?"

Pam kissed the back of my neck. "Uh-huh."

"Wha? I took an Ambien before I hit the sack, so I'm really groggy and gotta ask, are you fuckin' with my mind?"

She giggled.

The Pam I'd talked with before I went to bed wouldn't have said, "Be who you're supposed to be."

That's why I'd taken the Ambien. We had, before I fell into

bed, decided to separate.

It had been the end of a months-long process, the beginning of which was my telling Pam I might be trans. She was the first to hear the words come from my lips. Pam has long been an LGBTQIA+ advocate. Yet, it's one thing to support other people struggling for such rights. It's another when it drops a live shell into your marriage of nearly 31 years. One of her initial responses was:

> *You talk about shaving your beard and legs, wearing makeup, painting your toenails … and it's not that I'm opposed to those things in theory, it's just that it sounds so* not *you.*

How am I able to recall her words? Well—this is such a Pam-and-Bethany thing to do—we're both writers. We're also both articulate … but articulation is the first casualty in a marital conflict that could lead to relationship Armageddon. We've learned to commit such flammable thoughts to, um, well … a GoogleDoc.

Do *not* judge.

We can share it with each other, commenting back and forth, sans the looks of horror, revulsion, and *you-did-what?* In a GoogleDoc, we each can quietly digest the other's words, roll eyes, or shudder, and still absorb what the other is saying—without a knock-down, drag-'em-out, we-go-to-iHOP-at-4am-to-make-up-over-pancakes kind of blow up.

> Pam: *You and my brother are the two straightest guys I know. And though you may find the feminine beautiful and want to emulate it …* you are in no way *(outer appearance, demeanor, attitude) feminine.*

I'd told her I was exploring my feminine side, which I then thought serious enough a development to warrant that we discuss it via GoogleDocs. Here's part of that first GoogleDoc exchange:

<u>Me</u>: *What I'm feeling (and learning from my research), Baby, is that I have an internal identity with the feminine in the way a husband is attracted to his wife. To quote an article I read last night by Andrea Long Chiu: "The truth is, I have never been able to differentiate liking women from wanting to be like them."*

At this moment, I'm just asking myself "How should I live my life with this?" I'm learning about myself, and what I learn today can and will be changed by what I learn tomorrow. The only person I'm telling is you, 'cuz you should know what's going on. If you don't wanna know, I understand. This is making me re-examine everything about myself. I can't imagine what kind of impact it must be having on you.

Well, now, *that* made everything clear and easy-to-digest for my spouse! Here was Pam's very first reply:

This doesn't freak me out. That having been said, you feel this need to be honest with me about stuff … which is not so much a need to be honest, as a need for you to process aloud.

So, I know where you're at, and I prefer not to know the details—not because I don't love you or think it's weird, but because it's just not my thing to want to talk about that stuff. That doesn't mean, however, that you have to hide it from me. Fair?

For the next few weeks, the GoogleDoc exchange continued.

<u>Pam</u>: *So, despite the agreement to not talk verbally about your current situation, we still talk about it. You think that, if you say "I know you don't want to talk about it, but …" that we aren't really talking about it. But we are.*

Consequently, I have some thoughts to share:

Why does this happen around this time—the last two Januaries, and now this year? Part of me says, well, if this is a recurring theme, then it must be legit. But another part says, wait a tick … this happens at the time of year when you're least busy with work and have time to sit with your thoughts. Once things pick up again, it fades.

I'm not dismissing what you're thinking or how you feel. Yet, when I'm left alone with my thoughts, I create elaborate scenarios that evoke real emotions and real reactions, but, in the end, the scenarios are still illusions.

I want to give you room to be you. But it makes me uncomfortable because I simply don't see it. You talk about shaving your beard and legs, wearing makeup, painting your toenails … and it's not that I'm opposed to those things in theory, it's just that it sounds so not *you.*

Me: *You've ALWAYS let me be me. This is about exploring my heart more deeply. I've known, for literally decades, that I've been manning-up to compensate for something. I've been building a container or fortress.*

I never told you this, but I crossdressed a couple times when I was a teen. Just me and the mirror when no one was home. It felt good in a way that my teen brain couldn't express. When I was in utero, *my Mom, Dad, and brother were all certain that I was a girl and would talk to the womb, calling me "Beth Ann." I ain't saying this "made me what I am," 'cuz Correlation ≠ Causation, but there's a synchronicity there.*

Growing up, I lived in an environment where anything feminine was second-class—both at home and definitely in my community, in school, and with my peers. Though a loving father, my dad was a man's man, and my brother emulated that. I never engaged in the "player status" they did because I JUST DID NOT FEEL COMFORTABLE doing that—it was painful and utterly abhorrent to me. Though I've cultivated masculinity, I've never FELT AT HOME with it. My masculinity hasn't been a sham. It took charge in order for me to survive adolescence and young adulthood. Right now, I see myself as gender-fluid, profiling as a man but knowing I've got more under the hood, sore to speak.

Pam: *It's perfectly reasonable to want to get in touch with your feminine side. But that doesn't have to translate into picking out china patterns.*

Some of my best friends are incredibly sensitive, caring, insightful MEN (straight or gay). You don't have to be a girl to not be a Bro or douchebag. We're all more gender-fluid than traditional categories allow. I'm one of the least girly girls I know , but I don't confuse that with my being male.

Me: *I agree. That's one of the things I've always admired in you, Baby. There's a reason we're together. I didn't want/ need a girly female. You didn't want/ need a he-man. Deep calls unto deep.*

I'm not confused. I'm me and have a feminine side that deserves to be expressed—in a way that makes me happy.

There's a double standard that society allows for you but not for me—you can shave your hair down and get girly or manly tats, as you wish. You can be a non-girly female. But I can't be feminine without fielding embarrassment, shame, and accusations of deviance. Something of my outside needs to correspond with my inside. That would make me happy. What I'm exploring and learning about now are the ways in which I can do this and not only NOT damage our relationship but make it THRIVE even more.

Pam: *The last two Januaries show that you don't always think things through when you get in this frame of mind. You convince yourself you're "exploring" and enter into an alternative mindset ... until that fades. My concerns are that this feminine exploration the last two years led to things not thriving for us. I can't go through that again. Yes, I try to be the ever-supportive "you-do-you" partner. But that was really rough. I can't/ won't go through that again.*

Me: *And you won't have to. I am SO SORRY for that pain I caused you. That's why I need you in this. I'm not enlisting you as my voice of reason. Something is echoing in me. Do those echoes come from an empty shadowbox? Or is someone in that box begging for the light of day?*

<u>Pam</u>: *I don't offer these thoughts to dismiss, discourage, or embarrass you, but to show how it seems from my perspective. Can you at least promise not to shave the beard for a while? Yes, it's just hair and will grow back ... but let's put that to rest till mid-February.*

Even as I wrote these things to Pam, Bethany hadn't surfaced. My true self was the missing puzzle piece that had always been in front of me. I exhausted every other possible hiding place— under the bed, in the bathroom drawer, the car's glove box, religious faith, a devotion to literature, the pursuit of politics, throwing myself into marriage and fatherhood, being the good son to two flawed parents. It's not as if the puzzle piece didn't try to get my attention, in multiple ways. Here's one.

Three years prior to this round of feminine exploration, I had the most lucid dream of my life. In it, I was washing my face at the bathroom sink in the coldest, clearest-crystal water. When I looked in the mirror, I saw a gorgeous woman. I now realize that the reflection I saw was me as I am today. But back then, I didn't think I could *ever* look that way.

As the dream continued, I was made-up, dressed to the nines, and sitting in a parlor chair when a nondescript man entered the room and walked past me like I wasn't there. I was indignant that the guy didn't acknowledge how good I looked. After I woke, the dream lingered because I loved that I could feel that way. I felt righteous! I felt ... *right*.

Over the next week, I savored that feeling, whispering to myself, "I am a woman. *I* am a woman. I am a *woman*." My stomach leapt, and my heart thumped. I replayed that feeling till, eventually, the dream faded. Daily life exacted the toll of my having to be "Bob,"* groping for the missing piece of the happiness puzzle. To understand that journey, you need to know

---

*A family-favorite movie quote from *Orange County*, which quote we now use instead of my dead name, from the scene in which Catherine O'Hara's character refers to her latest husband "This new one ... 'Bob.'"

how "Bob" got to be "Bob," only to discover Bethany years later.

"Bob," not too long before events recounted in this book

Chapter 3

Fayettenam

Women's inequality is woven into men's identities in early childhood … Bleeding, leaking, seeping, oozing, and defecating are the stuff of our humanity and for this humanity, we particularly learn to revile women; and, as women, to hate ourselves.
—Soraya Chemaly, *Rage Becomes Her*

When I was a very small boy
Very small boys talked to me
Now that we've grown up together
They're afraid of what they see
That's the price that we all pay
And the value of destiny comes to nothing
I can't tell you where we're going
I guess there was just no way of knowing
I used to think that the day would never come
I'd see delight in the shade of the morning sun
My morning sun is the drug that brings me near
To the childhood I lost, replaced by fear
I used to think that the day would never come
That my life would depend on the morning sun
—New Order/"True Faith"

Long ago, on a birthday eve far away—August 21, 1975, to be exact—I felt the ravages of male-onset puberty.

And I didn't want it.

I didn't *know* I didn't want it.

I just felt so completely *wrong*.

My mother was an RN and had previously versed me in reproductive physiology and developmental changes. Why that was *her* job and not equally my father's, I don't know, but she took it on with vigor. The only sex education she got was after she had come home from school bleeding her menses, and my Nana gave my mom a belt and pads and told her to put them on once a month. Not one more word on the matter. My mom meant to make up in her children the deficiency of her own education in human sexuality.

Besides, it was the 1970s. People were "hip" with the whole sexuality thing (provided you weren't LGBTQIA+). So, when I was around seven years old and asked my mom innocent questions about boys and girls, geesh, I got a sawed-off-shotgun-barrel of information.

My mom's well-intentioned efforts had three problems:

1. She said nothing about the feelings that accompany the physiological changes. She told me that sometimes I might have dreams in which I got excited and woke up with a white substance emitted from my penis, but that it was nothing to be ashamed of. However, having been a bed-wetter till I was six years old, I knew a ton of shame surrounding what came out of my penis when I was in bed. Moreover, beyond saying "You can always talk with me or your dad about these things," she provided no apparatus as to *how* to talk with my parents about personal body-goo issues. No kid I knew of would ever feel comfortable broaching that subject with their parents.

2. She wasn't there when I hit puberty. She and my philandering dad were having marital problems. Again, though well-intentioned, they did a bang-up job of never evidencing their marital problems to me or my brother, Brian. So, imagine my shock when I was 10 years of age, sitting at the breakfast table spreading peanut butter on my toast and she asked, "Would you be okay if I wasn't here?"

    I hadn't woken too long before, I wanted to please her with a "right" answer, and I had no clue that this was her prelude to leaving me, so I answered, "Yeah, I guess."

    "Good," she said. "Because I won't be here when you come home after school."

I was demolished. But I knew not to show that to her. I could see by her demeanor that she couldn't handle any other response from me, as she then explained divorce about as clinically as she had sexuality. My mom could be like that—at a moment's notice an iron curtain slamming down, sequestering her from the feelings and concerns of any impacted by the decisions she unloaded on them.

After eating what I could of my toast and cereal, I went into my still-dark room, and, in the minutes before the school !bus arrived, cried my heart out. When I came home that afternoon, only my brother was there. I sobbed to him, asking "Why are Mom and Dad doing this?"

I had no clue at that moment that Brian was reeling as much as I was and had little more emotional equipage than I did to handle the shock of the situation. He did his best, though, and I'll always love him for that. He just kept saying to me, "I don't know. I don't understand it either."

3. Mom never said a damn thing to me about *how* puberty would happen—if there was a signal event. So, on the night of August 21, 1975, I was at a complete loss as to why I was feverishly rubbing my groin in such a way as to cause it to erupt and make me think I was dying.

     And that, folks, is the waaaay the news goes. Stay classy, Fayettenam.

I used to think that my mom's leaving was the first time I objectified my emotions. I simply stepped outside myself, watched myself feeling something, and, instead of actually *feeling* it, set it aside. Or, if the feeling was particularly intense, I held it at arm's length and turned it over, noting its features and the phenomena surrounding it, always making sure to tell myself that it wasn't really mine, as if it were the product of some external happenstance. At all cost, I was *not* to feel it. It wasn't my feeling to feel, wasn't my story to tell. Put it onto the dusty, high shelf with all the other specimens.

I'd been trained in objectification from so early an age that I'd no idea I'd become a master at it. My age-10 breakfast experience with my Mom was my Anakin-esque rite of passage from Padawan to Jedi status in the ways of objectification. My parents hadn't knowingly trained me in it, and I'd never requested it.

I'm not bragging when I say that I've always been cerebral. In fact, until recent years, I've held my being smart against myself, as it not only separated me from other, "normal" people, but it gave me the objectivity to *know* I wasn't normal. My parents later told me that, countless times when I was a small child and had said or asked them something, they exchanged glances, as if to say, "The kid's smarter than we are. What do we do?" Maybe that's why my mom felt no qualms telling me at a young age about sexuality or, over breakfast, informing me of her departure. She assumed my developed intellect made me *emotionally* equipped to handle and shelve such information downloads.

My dad treated my precociousness in a different way. I'd be outside or in the basement, playing, because that's where Dad was, working on fixer-up projects he enjoyed. Instead of the clinical redirection in which my mother specialized, my dad entertained my conjectures or even initiated discussions to which I could offer my cerebral two cents. Maybe he accepted that redirection was ineffective. Or, being a white male who enjoyed a world built for white males, he could speak what was on his mind and therefore saw no problem in engaging my queries. My mother, on the other hand, grew up in a world in which women were not encouraged to speak their minds. Being a nurse perhaps offered her a podium of expertise from which she could declaim with clinical certainty.

"Dad, what's a faggot?"

Most dads would've knee-jerk retorted, "Who the hell told you *that* word?"

My dad paused (perhaps thinking, "Jesus Christ, how do I answer that?" or "Does this kid have a turn-down-the-volume dial on *any* subject?") but then answered—choosing his words, 'cuz he knew I'd have no compunction about pontificating such wisdom to my peers.

"Well, Son, one meaning of that word is a tied-up bundle of sticks used to fuel a fire. I think it comes from the old English."

"Then why did Brian call Paul Lynde on *Hollywood Squares* a faggot?"

Longer pause while Dad fiddled with something on the workbench to buy time.

"I don't know where Brian got that—probably from one of his smart-aleck friends. It's a not-so-nice word for a man who acts effeminate." Which let me know that I shouldn't walk into my second-grade classroom and address my classmates with that particular epithet. If *Brian* said it about someone whom Brian obviously disrespected, then I should already know it was an insult. Dad volunteered only enough information to answer the question, which effectively put the subject on the shelf.

During my prepubescent days, I rarely let anything stay shelved. I'd wander my mind palace and pick items from the racks, turning them over, examining them, teaming them with disparate other items, and having jolly imaginative fun as only a weird, overly cerebral kid like me could. Except that I wasn't *just* cerebral. My emotions were all over the map. Think about Mr. Spock's childhood proclivities if he'd been reared by Dr. McCoy's parents. I was supplied all the information my parents thought I could handle. Yet, they were emotionally compromised, lugging their own baggage and hard-pressed to keep tabs on their own latent tendencies and motivations. Even if parents were issued a training manual, we'd need one for each and every kid, because each of us is a unique mystery—to ourselves, let alone to those who rear us. And what kid is equipped to understand that parents make it up as they go along? Say you find a stray duckling and feed it for a bit. Congratulations, you're now its momma G-d, at least in *its* mind. In parenting human hatchlings, you are G-d to your kid, with none of the omniscience to do the job justice. Sooner or later, the kid catches on.

Cerebral me *didn't* catch on … till that morning over toast.

Even before that, though, I was strong in the ways of objectification. When I was four, we moved to a home in a new subdivision. This was Southwestern Pennsylvania where the trees are humongous and verdant. Even though the copse of trees behind our home would soon give way to new houses in the subdivision, they were to me a children's edition of *Heart of Darkness.* I became obsessed with dinosaurs like Marlowe was obsessed with Kurtz.

Though my parents realized I was into T-Rexes, they couldn't guess how intensely I *felt* that pursuit. To them, as it would be to most parents, I was just interested in dinos. So they had no clue that, when I gazed at the woods outside my new bedroom, I was trembling like Bilbo Baggins at the prospect of traipsing into Mirkwood, which forest was populated not by Tolkien's giant spiders (also high on my list of things to fear) but by snarling, voracious thunder lizards from the depths of prehistory. When I offered tentative thoughts about the glowering jungle behind our new home, they would, with a mixture of clinical precision and the resourcefulness of giving me only the information needed to answer the question, reduce the woods to trees that were destined to be cleared and the biggest threat posed by which was poison ivy. "Remember—leaves of three, let it be."

I was worried about Buick-sized *toes* of three, but their matter-of-fact management of my hyperactive imagination taught me to do the same—namely, if I library it on the shelf of my mind palace, I can manage the fear. After playing in the backyard in the shadow of the trees, I walked inside the house and announced, "Mom, if you let dinosaurs alone, they'll leave you alone."

Out-loud pronouncements are my way of processing problematic phenomena, as if speaking my musings aloud will name and thereby exorcise the demon. My mom smiled to herself, affirmed my wisdom (having no idea that I was trying to reassure myself about the primeval jungle behind our house), and told me to wash my hands because dinner was ready.

On the shelf it went. My catalogue system, though, afforded no cross-indexing for the emotions involved. I'm not blaming my parents. Hell, I used to blame myself for being so damnably adept at objectification, therein affording my parents a mercy that I would, for the next four decades, not grant myself. Objectification was the means by which I attempted to cope with my parents' divorce and the onset of puberty.

In the weeks leading to my twelfth birthday, I'd been engaging in a new imaginative exercise in bed. The energies I'd used to process the possibility of Jurassic-era fauna in my backyard I now devoted to pubescent sexual fantasy. Though it was indeed the 1970s, when the sexual revolution was being cemented into the culture, all the taboos surrounding sex were not so easily dissipated in Fayettenam.

In my novel, *The Fire Golem,* Diana and Finn discuss the blighted economic and socio-cultural history of one Fayette County, nestled on the Mason-Dixon Line opposite West Virginia. That wasn't fiction, people. Fayette County has been economically, socially, culturally, emotionally, and spiritually depressed since before the Great Depression itself. This mountainous, river-threaded, forested region is a paradise for hunters, lumber companies, and Pittsburgh snow skiers and white-water rafters. It's hell to grow up there when you're a weird, cerebral kid. Education is not at the region's forefront of priorities. Yes, Fayette County boasted several school systems, but the prizing of education as a virtue was lacking. For what could it get you in Fayettenam? (By the way, I didn't come up with that moniker. It's an affectionate appellation used by locals whose own meager fondness for the environs is less than mine, with the added incentive that they're still locals there.) Education got you *out of* Fayette County. It had to. For, other than the school-systems and hospitals, employment and payoff were sparse for those who invested time, energy, and funds into getting educated.

I was held in awe by my classmates and teachers for being smart and using big words. But it was the awe reserved for carnival-show performers like Carl the Frogboy who annually appeared at the Fayette County Fair. "When you pass by this one, gawk, don't touch, then write it off as a freak." I literally terrified peers and educators who hadn't the modicum of coping skills my parents and brother wielded. We fear what we don't understand. And we hate what we fear. In the Fayette County of my youth, the culture and the school system granted little understanding and compassion. Though I was put into a box, I kept punching through, posing a challenge to those who prided themselves on contriving air-tight boxes.

For grades 4-6, I had some refuge in a stratifying educational innovation of the time. Dunbar Township Elementary school did something that might be unthinkable today, classing students in groups: The A-Group, B-Group, C-Group, D-Group, and E-Group, all assigned by academic performance—thus the letter-grade name of each group. What would be unthinkable now is that, not only did we kids *know* which group we were in but so did our parents and all the educators. What motivation did a kid have if they were plunked into the E-Group? And exactly what incentive did teachers have to treat them as anything other than a lost cause?

I was in the A-Group but didn't think I was hot shit for it, nor did most of its other members. We *liked* learning, partly because being in the A-Group sometimes made school interesting. I think the kids in the other groups pitied us for that. So, through my elementary years, I was being challenged and therefore tolerated school … to a point. I hated being herded around and being bullied, which I was, in spades.

Furthermore, even though I was in the A-Group, I was a freak there, too—though I wasn't singular in that. There were a few other kids who were freakishly smart and treated that way even by members of the A-Group. The thing was, the other designated "freaks" seemed reconciled to their status as the price of being smart. Also, for them, being smart meant knowing how to fly under the radar. If they were out-loud thinkers, they'd learned to tone it down.

I hadn't yet learned to ease my plane below radar level. Knowing that I was freakishly smart and therefore subject to derision in the Fayettenam milieu didn't incentivize me to tone it down. I was tolerated to the extent that all my teachers knew we were the A-Group and, as such, to expect smarts. As for the other kids in the A-Group, they, too, seemed to think it part-and-parcel that they were going to have some ersatz peers. They never held back on letting me know I was weird, but I gave as good as I got, and what I gave was armed with all the precociousness and none of the requisite charm that keeps you from getting beat up on the playground by the E-Group.

In elementary school, I didn't objectify my emotions about that bullying. I knew I was different, and I was proud of that. Did I feel bad that I was my own worst enemy, compounding my freak status by responding with more freakishness? Yes. But I didn't objectify my pain about that ... until doing so became self-preservation.

Puberty was rushing upon me, about to give me something I never knew I'd seek preservation from. Myself.

So, let's mix all this together into a pot. Precocious, weird kid. The onset of testosterone. A family in trouble. A setting that put me at the top of the heap without letting me forget my outsider status. Oh, yeah—having no clue I was trans. Last, a heaping helping of Fayettenam culture that prized size over smarts, brawn over burgeoning self-awareness, and titillating taboo over temperate understanding of what was happening to our ovaries, gonads, hearts, minds, and souls.

Starting in fourth grade, boys and girls would date or "go together," as was our now-antiquated parlance. That shit was daring in fourth grade, those who did so being held in reverence by the rest of us who hadn't a clue about *how* to "go with" someone. In fourth grade, I heard the first whispers of "Did you French her?" By sixth grade, it was "Did you fuck her?"

Those who answered these questions embellished their responses with outright lying, as, now in the light of experience, their reports of their extracurricular affections bear no credence as to their anatomical achievability. But who cared if it was bullshit? It was the *idea* of it all. By sixth grade, all of us guys, even in the pinheaded A-Group, had gawked at a *Playboy* centerfold released from the surly bonds of a dad's basement stash or older brother's mattress. By sixth grade, we all knew "faggot" meant a guy who liked other guys. How you physically expressed that attraction in the bedroom, if beyond some of our conceptions, was beside the point. If you couldn't show that you were manly enough to excel at sports, if you were in the least bit effeminate (or deemed so by your peers because you weren't as muscle-bound or hadn't yet "gone with" a girl), or if you were too fucking smart to be put in your place by wits, then you could be put in your place by heckling.

Despite the fact that going with a girl was a crown-jewel achievement, the most heinous words of disparagement were always voiced in terms of feminine-based derogative—"Pussy!" "Cunt!" "Bitch!" Even being called "fag" had less to do with the thought that you engaged in homosexual relations as it did with your being in some way like a girl. Not a single one of us ever thought about how this made the girls feel. I used these slurs and treated girls like shit. For to be friendly with girls (other than to be *going with* a girl) was itself an admission that you were feminine. So, I objectified the women around me, from my female peers to female teachers, celebrities, and media figures. To keep ahead of being heckled with slurs, I had to express interest in wanting to fuck a particularly good-looking female student and raucously accuse other guys of fucking the oldest, most objectionable-looking (to us) teacher or media figure (Phyllis Diller was considered a particularly heinous one in this category), or, at the lowest end of the totem pole, the most awkward, socially ungracious female peer.

That was a socio-cultural lesson in objectification. Despite my wanting not to fall into the slurred crowd (I already felt freakish enough), despite my growing hormonal attractions to girls, I felt, behind it all, an abhorrence at seeing girls this way. I honestly remember when first I was informed about coitus—I was flabbergasted that any woman would ever *want* that. It made me horribly shy about expressing interest in a girl, where my male peers wielded a facility (and no qualms whatsoever) in objectifying their female peers. As I headed into puberty, I also objectified something—my conflict between putting girls on a pedestal and the *use* of women as things to gratify sexual desire.

So, there I was … August 21, 1975 trying to go to sleep. It hadn't been the first time I felt the promptings that were keeping me awake. Though I knew I was sexually fantasizing, I didn't know *why* … other than, uh, that's what you do when images of that kind rush your brain and make you feel like you want more of them. As I wanted more, they kept coming more and more, building upon themselves and making me feel feelings I'd never felt before. And what young person can readily or accurately describe to themselves the primal experience of a feeling? I've felt desire a thousand million times since. But the brutal novelty of the feeling at its onset, combined with not knowing what was happening to me, was overwhelming. My functioning went autonomic. I knew dimly that I was rubbing the base of my scrotum and penis, but I didn't know why. It just *felt so damn good,* while simultaneously feeling like something that shouldn't feel good. I was thinking things not to be uttered aloud—you just feel them, but definitely don't talk about them. I knew from the dirty mags in my brother's room and the dirty talk among my classmates that what I was fantasizing was to be in hushed tones, behind dark velvet curtains, in seedy, grainy photographs. But I wanted it, wanted it badly till my body seized up. I thought I was dying. And I was alone. Dad was out dating. Mom was living 20 miles away. Brian was home, but he was in his room, listening to music on his headphones.

Though I tingled all over, something died in me that night. It had to. My body dictated it. And something was born in me. But I didn't have time to give it a name and no vocabulary to speak it, let alone someone to hear me out.

Someone hit the doorbell.

Holy shit!

Maybe Brian hadn't been on the headphones, because he'd

heard it and was getting the door. Who the hell comes over at 10:30pm on a weeknight? Probably some of his band mates.

He called my name. I jumped out of bed, threw on my pants, and came out to see Lucy and Carrie Myers, our next-door neighbors. Lucy was one grade younger than me and went to the Catholic school, while I was in public school. I remember her as being everything I prized in femininity—she was beautiful, innocent, and a sweetheart of a person. Her older sister, Carrie, was four grades ahead of me, already attending Catholic high school. Though she was pretty in her own way, she didn't have her sister's extraordinary natural beauty, but was every bit as good a soul and a talented artist to boot.

There they were, with presents, to celebrate my birthday. They'd thought of me and seemed utterly delighted at being able to surprise me and to see me open my gifts. They were going out of town the next day and wanted to give them to me as close to my birthday as possible.

I was floored.

"So, what have you been doing the night before your birthday?" Carrie asked.

What was I supposed to say? "Rubbing one out for the first time—here, let me shake your hand!"?

So much baggage for one stinkin' night.

Theirs, too, was a family fraying apart—perhaps why they'd reached out in kindness that night. One-and-a-half years earlier, their father, on Christmas Eve, no less, had, in his intoxication behind the wheel, killed a family of five just as they were turning into their driveway to kick off the holiday. I'll never forget all of my family there at the Myers' home, while their dad was in lock-up that night, with Lucy and Carrie kneeling beside their Christmas tree, sobbing. I remember so poignantly Lucy's ability to cry. I was numb. I guess I'd compartmentalized it, objectified it, for again, it was another new feeling for which I'd never been prepared. You heard about stuff like this on the news. Nondescript names, highway routes, fatal collisions in other townships. How to feel about it when it happened to two girls I played with on a daily basis and a family that had always been kind and generous to me? I remember poignantly Lucy's ability to *feel*. It awed me. I'd never wanted her in the way I callously talked with my classmates about Lynda Carter or Adrienne Barbeau ... until the time I couldn't stop looking at Lucy a certain way when she had come over to play Muppets with me a few weeks before.

Having grown up in a toxically masculine area in a household that, if it wasn't toxically masculine, nonetheless prized everything masculine to the near-total exclusion of the feminine, I knew implicitly from a young age that I was to be a boy. I'd no idea I could be anything else. I never hankered to wear Lucy's dresses or to play with dolls, but truth to tell, besides having a childhood crush on Lucy, I always felt more comfortable playing with her and Carrie than I did with the boys in our neighborhood.

Dad was the magnet in our household. Mom was chopped liver—till she wasn't there. My dad was a charismatic, winsome leading figure in our small city, looked up to by all the pillars of the community. He also was incredibly handsome and a consummately natural dancer. I didn't think about these things because I simply didn't see them as remarkable. He was Dad. And if my mom was a beautiful, talented woman, she was eclipsed in my eyes by my dad because she was always there for me at home. There when I woke up in the morning. There when I got back from school in the afternoon. There when I was sick. Which meant, of course, she was the one who more often than not taught and disciplined me. All the glory.

Brian and I waited for Dad to come home. Dad was fun. Dad knew the best games, the funniest movies, the most interesting things. In comparison, Mom (and, for that matter, my sense of my feminine self) was like a carton of milk in the fridge—you expected it to always be there for your cereal. Dad (and my need to be masculine in a way that ensured his staying in my life) was the prize inside the Quisp or Cap'n Crunch—you couldn't count on it being there, but when it was, you partied!

Everything on TV, at school, and in the world confirmed this bias. The masculine was supreme. It was shameful to throw like a girl. And, indeed, Lucy did throw like a girl. Not me. Nope. My dad had been a star shortstop in high school. He never was one of those Little-League dads, trying to make his sons into major-league material. But he played baseball with a grace and ease that I wanted to emulate. And he was a helluva batting coach, leading to priceless moments of father-son engagement when he'd take me and Brian to the lot next door or drive us to a nearby field to shag flies and ground balls and to, best of all, *hit*. Mom didn't know the measurements of a baseball diamond, let alone how to hit a frozen-rope liner. She knew medical stuff and was an expert on treating the scratches and bruises we'd get. But, hey, that was the milk you always expected to find in the refrigerator. Brian and I kept our eyes on the prize—Dad. So did the world around us, despite the Women's Lib movement, which, in Fayettenam, merited scoffing and derision. No wonder then, that I radically objectified any feminine tendencies in myself. I latched on quickly to the notion that being a dude was the ideal—no matter how much I nonetheless felt a pining admiration for the graces that Lucy could display so effortlessly, in just being herself.

She and I stood at the bus stop, with Carrie, on the last day of the school year, June 1975, about ten weeks before my August birthday. It was the last day of school, and I was crowing about it in my finest, every-thought-is-publishable form. I debated everything with Lucy and Carrie that morning, from whether Led Zeppelin (my top band at the time) was better than Paul McCartney and Wings (Carrie and Lucy's favorite) to the weather. Brian had armed me with snappy rebuttals that I gleefully flung at Carrie and Lucy. "Oh, please! Jimmy Page has forgotten more songs than Paul McCartney'll ever know!" None of my assertions had to be factual. I was a boy; they were girls. I merely had to declare it for it to be true. So, the discussion trundled from rock music to who had it better—Catholic or public-school kids.

Now, it was obvious to me at the time, even though my family was nominally Protestant, that Catholic school kids in that era got days off for any and every Feast. You couldn't sling a dead cat without hitting a Marian solemnity, and I'd stood alone at the bus stop on numerous occasions when Lucy and Carrie didn't have to go to school. But 11-year-old font-of-wisdom me was *not* going to concede a point to girls. I spun exaggerations and rationalizations that would've made a personal injury attorney gasp at my temerity and disregard for reality. I would simply not admit being wrong about the whole who-had-the-cushier-school-arrangement. I could hear the bus backfiring up the road long before it would appear to our eyes, when Lucy, fed up and righteously outraged as only a ten-year-old young woman can be, tore open my soul, to show me what I'd too many times objectified to avoid feeling.

"Randy Beeler, every time you cuss, every time you act so smart, every time you hurt my feelings, every time you treat yourself the way you do, you hurt G-d!"

She could muster nothing else because she was shaking and sobbing, Carrie with her arm around her. As the bus pulled up and the three of us got on, it was obvious to everyone that all was not right at bus-stop-ville. I felt eviscerated. It had been a painful but much-deserved emetic, and I could taste the bile of my existence on the last day of school, when I was supposed to feel the happiest, with summer ahead of me.

All summer. No Mom. No one to play with now that I'd shit on Lucy's soul. Dad out every other night on dates, with different beautiful young women. Me, hating myself for who I was and the things I was feeling. Never knowing *why* I hated myself. *Why* I felt the way I did. Because I'd put it all up on the shelf.

Lucy had busted the shelving unit and forced me to feel something for which I had no words but only raw feeling—a self-loathing so vast I couldn't see it. I'd hurt her, in a way I couldn't rationalize or trivialize … by just being me. The me I hated.

By my birthday eve, we had made up. There Lucy and Carrie stood, expectation in their eyes as I opened their gifts.

But Lucy had already given me a gift on that June morning.

Chapter 4

Going Under

"Finding yourself" is not really how it works.
You aren't a ten-dollar bill in last winter's coat pocket. You are also not lost.
Your true self is right here, buried under cultural conditioning, other people's opinions, and
inaccurate conclusions you drew as a kid that became your beliefs about who you are.
"Finding yourself" is actually returning to yourself. An unlearning, an excavation, a
remembering who you were before the world got its hands on you.
—Emily McDowell

The gift Lucy had given me was the gift to feel, without objectifying it. Her response was righteous and searingly raw, but Lucy didn't teach me to hate myself. I and circumstance had already done that. Hating ourselves is never ultimately true. It's a feeling jaundiced by our frustrations at not being what we set out to be. That's where the falsehood comes in. For what we think we *should* be is often fraught with illusion and unrealistic expectations. Being one with myself, *as* myself, was not something I was equipped to do when I was 11-going-on-12.

Middle school/junior high school is the hell hole of the educational system in our country. Educational administrators reform a school system from one end or the other, revamping first the primary or the high school modules. When, after five to six years, those reforms yield fruit, the reforming administrator gets promoted to a bigger, more rewarding position in a bigger, more rewarding school district ... just at the point when the educational reforms were about to reach the middle grades from one end or the other. Or, my analysis be damned, in the middle grades, maybe a preponderance of students and teachers are in some form of early-adolescent misery.

When I began seventh grade at Junior High West, I was translated from the refuge of the A-Group into a mix of everyone in every class. Gifted-and-talented program? *Ha!* As a seventh-grader, I was in the bottom-rung grade and regularly rubbed elbows with ninth graders whose two-years of advanced development dwarfed me. Beyond getting a report card, few gave a damn about academic achievement. Plaudits were reserved for jocks and popular kids. While I remained in a sixth-grade bodily frame, the girls around me, even the seventh-grade ones, were blooming physically.

Not only was I in the bottom-rung grade and bottom-rung of the President's Physical Fitness Challenge, I was at the bottom of the social ladder—underground, even. But I still kept opening my mouth like my pronouncements would evince everyone's appreciation of my intellectual prowess. That put a target on my back, not just for bullies but also for teachers who were much more consumed with crowd control than compassion. I was a square peg in all the round holes they'd carved to corral a hoard of hormone-dripping heathens. So, I became the pet project of those teachers who saw me as a threat to their authority.

Like calls unto like the Psalmist says. Though I know gifted, literally saintly educators who *purposely* teach middle grades and work true miracles, they are the exception. Although I didn't wake up each morning plotting how to piss off my teachers, some acted towards me as if they'd caught me laying land mines for them. As I said, I was not one to back down from a challenge, giving as good as I got. However, I was just trying to survive. I was literally *body slammed* into a hallway granite floor by a bully who was a good two heads taller. His girlfriend upbraided him, then tried to console me, which only put a bigger target on my back. Another hoodlum worthy of a lead role in the *Blackboard Jungle Reboot Meets Children of the Corn,* would, without warning, karate-kick my solar plexus or wing sharp objects in my direction. One time I was at the urinal, and this darling (who in intervening years did time in maximum security) launched a Kung-Fu kick to my back, leaving me unable to walk for 10 minutes. I had no means of reprisal against the goon squad. But with a teacher? There are all kinds of retaliations at the disposal of a smart kid bored with the standard crowd-control curriculum.

Viola Bordas was the last of a dying breed—a literal old-maid teacher who was looking to ride out her retirement year but who hadn't the grace to go gentle into that good night. She seemed appalled that I didn't get the memo that, no matter how smart I was, smarts shouldn't matter when someone has power over you. What she miscalculated was that I'd nowhere to go. I hated myself. Things at home were hideous (more on that ahead). I took my life into my hands walking the hallways or going to the restroom. The girls I worshipped regarded centipedes with more affection than they ever sent my way.

Wilson Fisk, aka the Kingpin, notes in *Daredevil: Born Again*, "And I have shown him that a man without hope is a man without fear." This, after he's discovered Daredevil's secret identity and literally destroyed his known world—but not succeeded in killing him. Let's just say that would-be Kingpin Bordas showed me that a self-loathing pubescent smart-ass without a vent is a person without scruple. I also knew I was smarter than her. She made it her personal, Wiley-E.-Coyote mission to prove otherwise. Miss Bordas, though 61 in earth orbits, had the emotional-development capacity of the students she was teaching, maybe less. She also didn't have the arm-strength to make her paddle a deterrent. (Remember? I told you this was *Fayettenam*. Any teacher who could toss a potato chip used corporal punishment.)

Nor did I take her in-class disparagement and bullying of me as anything more than incentive. While she'd pace us through eighth-grade grammar, something I already knew inside and out 'cuz I was reading at a college level, I'd write poetry or draw. She'd snatch my poems and artwork and read/show them to the class, who didn't bat an eyelash because they already knew I could write poetry and draw like crazy. Not only did this not embarrass me, it actually published my work, which, though not an advantage, given the junior-high audience, nonetheless brought me great personal satisfaction.

Miss Bordas gave us mindless homework assignments, such as "Use and underline each of the following words in a grammatically correct sentence." So, I took the word, "infamous," from the list, and buried it in sentence #7, which read "Miss

Bordas is <u>infamous</u> for her mind-numbingly boring homework assignments."

I kid you not, during a passing period as students flooded the hallway, she ran out of her room and accosted me for daring to write such a sentence. I was thrilled.

Changing her tactics, she gave Will Orson a sentence to read aloud from our grammar book: "I spilled ink on my dress."

Will was no dummy. He just shut up, acting like he didn't hear her. So, Miss Bordas called on me to read it, a mousy smirk on her face, while Will guffawed, "Yeah, that's more like Beeler's kind of sentence!"

This aggression would not go unchallenged. I thought quickly and read aloud, "I spilled ink on Will's dress," bringing down the class in laughter. She didn't call on me for a week.

On another occasion, she was pacing us aloud through a fill-in-the-blank series of sentences in which students had to pull out of thin air an appropriate simile to complete the sentence. The one she gave me read "He laughed like _____," which I promptly completed with "He laughed like <u>a constipated</u> <u>hyaena</u>." Cue classroom laughter and plaudits.

That one got me sent to the vice-principal's office, where Mr. Zavatsky, veins popping in his throat, demanded, "Do you even know what a constipated hyaena laughs like?"

It was all I could do to keep from laughing, and I wasn't constipated.

None of this gained me ground with my other teachers, my report card, and least of all, my peers. Unlike elementary school, I was not just a freak, but I was painfully aware that I could be nothing else. And home was no sanctuary, as I was treated like a freak there, too.

My father was a *playah*, and the gene passed on to Brian, as well, who had a drop-dead gorgeous girlfriend, whose lack of brains and common sense Brian didn't mind a bit. My father, on the other hand, dated beautiful women *with* intelligence. The one with whom he fell in love, Laura, had, believe it or not, been my Kindergarten teacher in her very first year of teaching (yup, I welcomed 'em in and retired 'em out).

After the dust had cleared from my parents' divorce, I was given the choice of who I wanted to live with. My dad retained the house, which kept me in the same school. Though I'd no great love for Junior High West, I did have my only friends there, my room and the house (now dinosaur-proof) in which I'd grown up … and Dad. *I had Dad.* Brian had lived there through my dad's singles interim, but he was commuting to college and sowing his wild oats. *I* counted myself as the one who'd stuck with Dad and seen him through difficult times. I'd witnessed sides of him that I hadn't before guessed at—the loneliness and stress, the harrows of the divorce. I saw my dad in a way that few, if any, had seen him—imperfect, flawed, vulnerable, needy, uncertain. And I loved him all the more for it, 'cuz I was his kid. I was thrilled that Laura took to me with vigor and attention. It was obvious she adored Dad, so she was doing everything to extend love to me. I wholeheartedly gave a thumbs up on their union, as if it ever were anything for me to decide.

It's a lot easier to love a person's kid when you're dating that person. What happens, though, when you get married and come 24/7 into a home that had been the setting of his previous marriage, with his two sons there as constant reminder that this ain't your turf, but theirs? Further, Laura brought her own baggage, having seen her father abuse her mother. My dad was her be-all and end-all, her knight-in-shining-armor. He was mine, too. And I thought I was his trusty squire. But the armor had dents in it and couldn't bear a tug-of-war between his child and his new bride.

Laura had no experience in living in a home with a 21-year-old aspiring-rock-star guitarist and his troubled kid brother. Add to the mix that she and Dad were not getting on as cozily as they'd anticipated. She fell into what I now surmise was anxiety and depression at not being able to make her home and marriage what she wanted. My dad was clueless as to how to ameliorate the problem. I know, because he had little compunction sharing his marital woes with me. He'd landed her. He'd made a home with her. He got the stability back that he'd longed for. What gave?

Laura focused her efforts first on Brian, eventually getting my dad to move Brian's things to the front porch, kicking him out. She next turned on me. One Saturday morning, she literally took my bedroom door off its hinges, accusing me of slamming it and keeping her awake in the morning. She then got my dad to convert the garage, on the other end of the house, into a new master bed and bath, so they could keep their bed far away from me. (Okay, I can understand that one.) She berated me, called me names, insulted me, treated me like a second-class citizen. The same way I'd responded to Miss Bordas, I answered Laura. I even let my dad triangulate me into talking to her when she was her most depressed and carrying their child, my half-brother. What a hideous position that put the two of us. Her, with morning-sickness ravages of a first pregnancy. Me, with my self-hatred and the hell of junior high. We were nitro and glycerin, and my dad was doing everything to not be a casualty.

Laura convinced my dad that she had to have my room as the nursery for my half-brother. This had been *my room* for ten years. It caught the sun from both the south and the west, and I lived for the sunshine. I was moved to Brian's old room that caught no sun whatsoever and still smelled of the incense he'd burned to cover pot smoke. The day they'd moved me into there had been a rough one, and, as I lie in bed, I heard Laura vituperating about how ungrateful and awful I was. I realized then that I'd lost the battle for Dad ... which I hadn't known was a contest in the first place. I cried my eyes out and begged the universe, "Please. Help me." The poison of testosterone was running in my veins, making my body change in ways that I now realize were abhorrent to me but back then only filled me with no clue where it was leading. My dad was the foundation of masculinity on which I'd built my self-image as the faithful son. But that foundation was of sand.

I'd objectified it all, for it hurt too much to live with. There was no internet accessible to me in the 1970s wherein I could gather some explanation about why I felt so estranged from my own body, dissociated from the feminine I intuitively gravitated to, and betrayed by a masculinity alien to my sense of self. I didn't grasp that my derision of the feminine was the internalized root of my self-loathing. I fell into swooning crushes on girls at school but felt paralyzed to act upon them, because when I did, I was rejected. The feminine that was my true self had gone under at the onset of male puberty. I now suffered the latent anxiety, depression, and despair of being separated from who I truly was. My birthright had been stolen, with my aid and acquiescence, because I'd never known it was mine in the first place.

I'd fallen into a cyclical pattern—battling the women in my life for what scraps of dignity were left to us. Lucy. Miss Bordas. Laura. Every girl I placed on an impossible pedestal, who then reeled at what must've seemed my inordinate and unasked-for worship. I had nowhere to go but up. At one time in my life I would've told you that, indeed, this was my low point. But I stayed under. I went sideways and mistook movement for upward progress.

Eight Grade: I'd Won the Wacky-Day Dress-Up Contest—'Twas Fitting

Chapter 5

Sideways, With A Dose of Religion

Don't do this and don't do that
What are they trying to do?
Make a good boy of you
Do they know where it's at?
Don't criticize, they're old and wise
Do as they tell you to
Don't want the devil to
Come out and put your eyes

Maybe I'm mistaken expecting you to fight
Or maybe I'm just crazy, I don't know wrong from right
But while I am still living, I've just got this to say
It's always up to you if you want to be that
Want to see that want to see that way
You're coming along
—Richard Davies & Roger Hodgson/"School"

Human beings are cyclical creatures, forming patterns of meaning that grant us certainty and foundation. Done right, our cycles form an upward spiral. We return to the same side of the mountain but at a higher perspective. Sadly, the endeavor doesn't always turn out that way. Some of us go in circles in the dark, trying to reassemble the puzzle pieces of the past into a present picture that grants a future of hope. In such moments, even the dimmest light makes us think we see the whole picture and march ever upward. But we're moving sideways, convincing ourselves that this turn around the mountain is indeed at a higher vantage.

That night of desperate realization, having lost the battle for Dad, was indeed a low point—but not one that I permanently squared in the rearview mirror. I would return to it so long as I remained unaware of my true self. But I had to start up the mountain somewhere, even if it meant carving a rut in the same orbital path for years and calling it my highway to heaven.

Some rescue came in the form of testosterone stabilization. Hormones leveled off. I was still as horny as a springtime rabbit, but the first-time feelings created by puberty became a norm that, if I hadn't asked for them, were something that, by their continued presence, made me shrug, "I guess this is life."

That was a theme to dog me the next four decades. Trans persons who don't realize their trans identity till after adolescence describe their situation (undiagnosed gender dysphoria) in the same way I summarize those 40 long years: I *ached* with an existential malaise I couldn't pin down. Wholeness, balance, contentment, and *being at home with myself* were always out-of-reach. And *anger*. Always the anger. Simmering, sometimes popping the lid of the hermetically sealed container I built. Anger that, "Damn it! I've shut out my sunlight again!" So, I would smash shelves and climb up the rubble to where I could pop a chink through the battlements, and, for a time, breath fresh air like I was on the mountain peak. I could *see* … people leading their lives like the gifts they are. I mistook my peephole glimpse for my being one of them, free to move about. The ones unencumbered with self-hatred I tagged as members of a tribe I had to join. I became a model tribe member, to the point that I confused being *in* a tribe for living as my true self. I built fortress after fortress in the image of one tribe after another … always wondering where my sunlight went.

Holing up in my dark room with a volume of Tolkien or C.S. Lewis and old Genesis vinyls playing was my refuge. These artists took me to another place in which virtue was a real thing. In which hatred and evil could be overcome with persistence and humble courage. It was a different library, one for which I've always kept open every window, wall, and door. One of my few regular outings was to a tiny youth group at Dunbar Presbyterian Church, where my dad had become active. This was not a rabid, evangelical, fire-and-brimstone church. Its youth contingent was a half-dozen middle-school kids like me (and, of course, I was crushing on one of the girls in the group). So, I went to Sunday services and, at age 14, was confirmed in the PCUSA. But, really, that mainline-Protestant congregation didn't fuel my embrace of

Christianity so much as did C.S. Lewis … whose *Chronicles of Narnia* had been recommended to me by the female pastor's 16-year-old daughter on whom I also was crushing.

Lewis stuck. A quote of Rabindranath Tagore (that's incorrectly attributed to Gandhi) goes, "Jesus is ideal and wonderful, but you Christians, you are not like him." Lewis is like that. I wish more Christians would be like Lewis, who had a rapier wit and refreshing spontaneity. I already had latent Anglophilia; Lewis sealed the deal. Any person who can limit themselves to two pints of ale as a Lenten penance is my kind of believer. I moved from *Narnia* to Lewis' *Space Trilogy* to *The Screwtape Letters*, *The Great Divorce, Till We Have Faces,* then to his nonfiction—*Mere Christianity, The Problem of Pain, The Abolition of Man,* and the haunting memoir of his wife's death, *A Grief Observed.*

"This was *Fayettenam!*" she hollers for the third time. I was reading the works of an Oxford and Cambridge Professor of Literature while I hauled ass to school, dodged bullies, adored girls from afar, and survived gym class. In ninth grade (top stratum of the junior-high ecosystem, baby!), I got into a newly formed Advanced Art class that was the closest thing Junior High West had to the A-Group. I painted, drew, and wrote poetry, free of the surly bonds of the freshly-retired Miss Bordas. It wasn't paradise. I was still a bottom-feeder in that top-rung pond, but I began to make headway against the current. One day, as I sat in class, early in my ninth-grade, I realized, "Holy shit! If I just stop being a smart-ass with no restraint and flick my intellectual wrist, I'll have these teachers eating out of my hand. I'll be one of the grade-grubbers, but at least I'll belong to some tribe."

The grade-grubbers didn't get harassed as much, as if the bullies had murmured, "Those bookworm bastards are so sorry that no amount of knuckles will rescue them." It wasn't a group, per se, but, if you kept your nose clean in class (i.e., no references to the bowel irregularities of any African mammal), answered questions correctly, turned in sterling work (which wasn't hard), and helped other students, the predators would see you as an egregiously untasty species in the junior-high habitat and let you alone.

I still wore a target, but now that a few teachers had my back and I was no longer a crowd-control issue for the administration, I could stand up to the bullying. Ninth grade is the first year of high school, even if you're in junior high. The bullies' day was passing. Those hoods were already, in the esteem of the greater schooling ecosystem, being parsed out as druggies, juvenile delinquents, and ignorant assholes. *They* were the ones who were beginning not to fit into the society for which the American education/socialization apparatus was fashioning us. Another brick in the wall, another drone in the hive mind, another cell in the cultural corpus. All the same to me, as I was no longer getting Kung-Fu kicked at the urinal.

Belonging to the smart-kids club and being passed over by the administrative stormtroopers enabled me to set aside self-loathing for the time being. I still knew I wasn't the shit, but it made me feel a little like Éowyn (my favorite character in my favorite book, *The Lord of the Rings*) to stand up to my oppressors. I can relive down to the dark-matter level my first encounter with Éowyn. She is bad-ass enough to put *Aragorn* in his place:

> *"All your words are but to say: you are a woman, and your part is in the house. But when the men have died in battle and honour, you have leave to be burned in the house, for the men will need it no more. But I am of the House of Eorl* and not a serving-woman. *I can ride and wield blade,* and I do not fear either pain or death" [emphasis mine].

That alone had me head-over-heels in love with her. Galadriel and Arwen were like all the girls out-of-my-league—beautiful to admire but inaccessible to hairy-footed hobbit *moi*. Éowyn is crushed by her female second-class social status. Stalked by Grima Wormtongue. Neglected by her uncle, King Theoden. Unrequited by Aragorn. Loathes her station even though she tries to rise above it, passing as the soldier, Dernhelm, to sneak into battle. While rising above it, she lowers a hand to hairy-footed hobbit Merry, empowering him to share her adventure. When that leads them to face the Nazgûl King, Éowyn does not succumb to his witchery, but *laughs* at him!

"Begone, foul dwimmerlaik, lord of carrion! Leave the dead in peace!"

A cold voice answered: 'Come not between the Nazgûl and his prey! Or he will not slay thee in thy turn. He will bear thee away to the houses of lamentation, beyond all darkness, where thy flesh shall be devoured, and thy shriveled mind be left naked to the Lidless Eye."

A sword rang as it was drawn. "Do what you will; but I will hinder it, if I may."

"Hinder me? Thou fool. No living man may hinder me!"

Then Merry heard of all sounds in that hour the strangest. It seemed that Dernhelm laughed, _and the clear voice was like the ring of steel._

"But no living man am I! You look upon a woman. Éowyn I am, Éomund's daughter. You stand between me and my lord and kin. Begone, if you be not deathless! For living or dark undead, I will smite you, if you touch him." [emphasis mine]

She and Merry then together dispatch Sauron's second-in-command. Utterly bad-ass. Did I mention that I held Tolkien in as high esteem as Lewis?

Not only did I stand up to bullies, but I actually went with a girl. To this day, I don't know whether she understands what a huge ray of sunlight she brought into my life for a few short months in the spring of ninth grade. She liked me. Enough to publicly go with me. Holy Schneikes! But a problem still persisted. I was terrified of kissing her. So, I didn't. She was eminently kissable. I was terrified, though, that I'd screw it up. So, I didn't, and the romance fizzled out. I'd graduated from putting a girl on a pedestal to actually daring to get up there with her. But I got only so far as a "you can look but you no can touch" approach. The feminine was still unattainable to me.

Nonetheless, I had confidence, a tribe (Christian grade-grubbers), Junior High West in the rearview mirror, and even resolution of my hideous home situation. Rising from the dregs that was Junior High meant that, for my Sophomore through Senior years, I'd attend Connellsville Area High School. Laura and my dad had decided to sell our home and move to a new place in a neighboring school district that may have been even more Fayettenam than was Connellsville. However, my mom still lived in the Connellsville school district. Voilà! I moved in with her and my stepdad, Bill, for my high-school years. I transferred my gig to a new location but kept the same moves—introverted, into fantasy/sci-fi and prog rock, keeping my under-the-radar profile in school with the more-or-less holy academic types. No more youth group, but, myeh, I had Lewis, and I read the entire Bible cover-to-cover.* I excelled in my college-prep classes and indeed thought I was the shit academically. No more bullying. I made some new friends who once hailed from Junior High *East*. Best of all, in the spring of my Junior year, I got a girlfriend whom I actually kissed. A lot.

Miri didn't go to my high school but to one in next-door Westmoreland County. She was sweet, in love with me, and I with her. Her mom, however, was hyper-vigilant about sexuality, maybe even obsessive. Her idea of Miri and I dating was that we stay at home in the living room of their house while she and Miri's dad kept their bedroom door open.

Miri and I were both Bible-believing Christians, except that, like so much of evangelical notions of sexuality, we got everything wrong. It was a new level of "you can look but you can't touch," but more like "we can touch here but we don't put it *there* or the Lord will smite us." It was a recipe for futility and the demise of our relationship. We hung on together, even when I went to my first year of college at the University of Dallas in Irving, TX, but the summer after that saw Miri break up with me. In later years, I told Miri that she'd done a courageous thing in calling us off. She'd needed to get out from under the watchful eye of her mother, and going to Texas, for her, was not an option. Moreover, I put her on a pedestal as I'd done with other girls. So, we never "did it." Part of that was our preference, but most of it

---

*I don't recommend it unless you need a cure for insomnia; it ain't a novel and deserves to be read in terms/order of only the books for which you have a specific interest. It ain't a rulebook, for Chrissakes. Even Jesus didn't read the Torah from cover to cover. He heard parts of the Torah and Prophets read aloud, in Synagogue.

was *me*, despite the fact that, after every date I felt like I could pole vault home. I had this objectified, on-the-highest-shelf ideal of the feminine that I subconsciously was trying to preserve. And I was stubborn … to the point of being a frustrated (and frustrating) prick. Remember how I treated poor Lucy? You would think I learned my lesson with *Making Girls Cry*, the movie. I made the second, third, and fourth sequels with poor Miri, with maybe even a prequel thrown in.

I remember one winter date with Miri that exemplified my underlying trans self that I steadfastly refused to see. Miri lived in the valley; I lived at my mom's, in the nearby Laurel Mountains. By the time I was ready to leave Miri's at 10pm, a snowstorm had rolled in, and Miri's mom, of all people, urged me to spend the night on the living-room sofa sleeper (Miri ensconced in her bedroom, of course, her parents keeping their bedroom door open). Miri and I were on the sofa sleeper, saying goodnight, when I hugged her with all my might, like I was melding myself with her. Though I had no conscious awareness of it at the time, I know now that something deep inside me wanted what Miri had—femininity, grace, the ease of being herself. Miri had those in spades and shared them with me for two years plus. For that, I'll always be grateful to her.

Sideways onward I went after my post-first-year-of-college summer's break-up. That fall was my Rome semester. You can't really grasp the University of Dallas (UD) unless you've attended there. Costeen Brave, the hero of my novel, *Maria (of the angels)*, describes it in better words than I can here. The place is *intense*. And extremely Catholic. A pioneer of the study-abroad program, UD had its own campus in Rome and was definitely not a blow-off, let's-fling-our-parents'-cash-across-Europe study-abroad semester. Virtually every Sophomore, in either Fall or Spring, attended UD in Rome. UD had a core curriculum in which, regardless of your major, everybody, and I mean *everybody*, took the same 60 credit hours in the Western Intellectual Tradition—Literature, History, Philosophy, Theology, Political Philosophy, foreign language, sciences, Art History, Math, and more. The core courses in Rome dovetailed with Classical Antiquity, the Middle

Ages, and the Renaissance. We literally learned on-site about Greek drama in the amphitheater at Epidaurus, Roman history in the Forum and Pantheon, early Christianity in the Catacombs, the Franciscan Movement in Assisi, and the Renaissance in Florence.

The UD experience is an education that, to this day, enables me to know and wield far many things beyond my major. It taught me how to learn … *anything*. UD's marketing motto is "The University for Independent Thinkers," and I'd like to believe that this immersion into the Catholic liberal arts tradition truly made me independent. But actually, all who attend UD bring their own nascent independence with them that UD nurtures, for there's another side to UD that has gotten only more intense (and not so independent) to this day—its tribal Catholicism. UD ain't just *in* the Catholic tribe. It sees itself as the one non-loose wheel on the entire Catholic parade float, including that of the Pope.

In Rome, I went sideways with the religion thing again. Also, with my dating thing. Again.

In Rome, I fell in love with Catholicism.

In Rome, on the sideways rebound, I also fell in love with Felicia, who, as it turns out, was not so in love with me. She and I had what UDers call a "Rome-mance." Falling in love with Felicia, I pulled off what I hadn't with Miri—melding faith with my suppressed hunger for my female self. Like Miri, Felicia was a sweetheart, and a hearty traveling companion. She was also a conservative Catholic from a conservative Italian-American Catholic family—so "you can kiss, but you no touch-a nuthin' else." It was like kissing statues of the Virgin Mary (though, admittedly, more responsive). And I don't mean that flippantly about Felicia or sacrilegiously about the Mother of God.

The Marian Cult in the Catholic tradition is the Goddess' "minority report."† It's like Whack-A-Mole, except it's Pray-A-

---

†Prior to 3,000 years ago, humanity lived in cultures of partnership between women and men, with the Goddess enshrined as the expression of this partnership and humanity's close ties to the natural world. The collapse of the Minoan civilization in ancient Crete marked the last of those partnership cultures to succumb to the conquering, male-dominant tribes. You can see this history written in the war-based migrations of the Egyptian, Sumerian, Mycenaean,

Mary. Marian apparitions and adorations come at crisis times for church and civilization, the iron-fisted male-dominant society generating a longing for what is missed—the complementarity and partnership exemplified by the mother Goddess. Post-crisis, the male overlords grudgingly admit the feminine *can't* be erased; so, boys, let's put her in a nook in every church—a desperate form of Whack-A-Mole. They drape the machine with their bodies, only to get popped in the groin. ††

Curious how this trend mirrors my bottling my female self.

UD, Felicia, and Pray-A-Mary took me by storm. Here was not only a tribe in which I could grade-grub with impunity, but I could exorcise my testosterone demons via heterosexual marriage. And I could bully those who weren't part of the club!

Except that, when we got back to main campus for the Spring semester, Felicia dumped me.

So, I would out-g-d G-d. I would become a priest, damn it! … Then Pam entered my life.

Just a dude posing as if alone with his thoughts during his Rome semester.

Dorian, Hittite, and Israelite peoples. Since that time, our collective lives have been based on a model of conquering, thunder-fisted male gods, with men dominant over women. Religion to this day maintains this male-dominant hegemony. But the minority report still makes its way to the surface. In Catholicism, Mary is the minority report that arose after the early-church councils and Rome's adoption of Christianity banned the equalitarian presence of women in church life and leadership that had been nascent Christianity.

††This has its equivalents in other cultures and religions that subjugate the feminine.

Chapter 6

Pamalyn Tonic

I owe my relationship with Pam at least in part to C.S. Lewis.

Pam was an incoming Freshman at UD when I was a rising Junior. (*Of course* I scammed on the newbies.) I attended the Freshman-Orientation Book-and-Movie Discussion because it involved two authors I love—C.S. Lewis and Flannery O'Connor. The orientation team showed John Huston's cinematic adaptation of O'Connor's novel, *Wiseblood,* and assigned the incoming Freshmen Lewis' *The Abolition of Man,* as a lens through which a professor panel would engage them in Q&A baptism by fire. Post-movie, nary a Freshman raised their hand at the profs' opening question. Remember that I was the junior-high student who had coined a simile between laughter and constipated African scavengers. I was born for this moment. Hell yes, I raised my hand. Seeing no Freshmen rise to the bait, the prof panel called on me to spin some fodder. I don't recall what I said, but, as the Freshmen warmed to the task, I heard a female voice quoting *me* by name. A young woman adumbrating eloquently about my input on the matter at hand snagged my attention. After was a watermelon mixer (standard UD fare was wine and cheese, so this was a welcomed novelty), during which I approached the lady quoter-of-me and asked how she knew my name.

Turns out, she'd made friends with Emma, a Freshman I'd earlier met (and scammed on—never underestimate the power of "I'm discerning the priesthood" at a Catholic school*). Emma had acquainted her with my name as I answered the panel's initial question, and Pam took it from there, she, the watermelon, and our subsequent conversation hitting on all cylinders. What is so

---

* After her Freshman year, Emma became a nun in the Daughters of St. Paul; so, yeah, also never *over*estimate the power of a potential calling to the priesthood.

refreshing about Pam is how utterly *real* she is. After the first five minutes, I forgot the watermelon. After two weeks, I responded to religious vocation queries with "Huh? There's a priesthood?"

I must've intuited that Pam fit together my scattered pieces. But she steadfastly avoids placement on a pedestal and emits a fire that vaporizes bullshit, which I was peddling to myself in those days. I truly hadn't been scamming on Freshman girls—I was discerning the priesthood, my feminine self be damned. Pam assured me, "You'd never be happy as a priest." Instead of harping on whether I was "called" or the theology behind the question, Pam focused on my happiness. I'd so long objectified my feelings that I wouldn't have recognized happiness had it kissed me under the moon on a tree-lined path, which Pam did when I finally had enough sense to ask her out. That path was on *Seminary Hill*, no less, the Seminary itself down the hillside.

My G-d, she is a babe.

I, too, had uncanny insight into what impassioned her, as well as displaying in her presence an integrity I'd not previously wielded. Through the years, she has steadfastly countered my objectifying tendencies, her very person challenging me to feel what I'm truly feeling, even when those feelings are messy. I was more than smitten. In two months, I knelt on the floor of the chapel confessional where we were macking out and asked her to marry me. To my utter astonishment, she said "Yes!"

But ours hasn't always been a happily-ever-after journey.

Pam lives to intuit people's expectations of her and deliver on them in gift-basket loads. When age-four Pam was with her mom in the mall, her mom said, "I'm going to look in that shop over there. Sit on this bench and don't move a muscle till I come back. I won't be long." These were the days when the world was safe enough to do this kind of thing with your kids. Her mom kept her eye on Pam all the same, which leads to the punchline—Pam literally did not budge a muscle. Didn't swing her legs. Didn't glance around. She must've breathed because she's still here today, but even that movement wasn't discernible to her mom as she relieved Pam's vigil on the mall bench.

Ninety-nine percent of the time, Pam's meeting of expectations is tremendously winsome and makes people feel like they're the center of her attention, which indeed they are. However, the one-percent exception are those rare individuals whom Pam can't read because: (1) they aren't communicating (implicitly or explicitly) their expectations; or (2) they are intentionally or unintentionally frustrating Pam's attempts to deliver on what she thinks they expect. My objectification tendencies occasionally served up one or both of these Pam-doomsday scenarios. I didn't push these buttons all the time, or we wouldn't have made the relationship last six weeks. Yet, I didn't *know* when my emotional signal-to-noise ratio was crackling with interference. Gender dysphoria (especially given I didn't *know* that such was my problem) created an emotional dissonance whereby I didn't know *how* I was supposed to feel. Add to that my objectification of problematic emotions to craft a recipe for ill-communication. I didn't just short out her expectation radar— hell, I didn't even know what *I* expected or what *to* expect in terms of life fulfillment. I chased tribal identities and forged a resilient container that rendered me clueless to the me inside it. Had I succeeded, I would have permanently shut me off from me, rendering myself a fitter candidate for psychopathy than for the priesthood, husbandhood, or fatherhood.

The funny thing about relationships is that they aren't meant to be ideal. A healthy, curative relationship can sometimes make you wanna die. The opposite of a toxin (a poison that disrupts or destroys the functioning of an organism) is a tonic—a catalyst that enlivens and innervates. Yet, it's not that tonic relationships don't cause disruption—oh, hells to the yes, they *do!* Relationship tonic works like physical exercise—literally tearing down body structures to build a stronger organism. No pain, no gain. I'll again drag in C.S. Lewis, who saw mercy as often necessarily disruptive. "Severe mercy" is a hindsight realization after we exit the tunnel in which we'd cursed our fate but now see that we wouldn't *be* in the light if not for that dark journey. It's severe when we're going through it and a mercy only after we've become the new person that severity has created. I'm not saying "hard shit builds character," because evil, misfortune, and plain stupidity too often *destroy* character (remember the toxins I referred to above?). Mercy, however, is the tonic that rescues.

Why have Pam and I been tonic for each other when my previous relationships ended toxically? If I could bottle the answer, I wouldn't be writing this book but honchoing the world's largest pharmaceutical concern. Somehow, Pam and I so grace each other. When Pam and I rubbed each other the wrong way, we didn't cause spiritual and emotional third-degree burns but started a fire that, instead of consuming us, sustains, renews, and gives life, if our three adult kiddos are any indication.

I was intent on sealing away the real me. As a matter of personal faith and the evidence of my own experience, I believe the cosmos is built on the dark matter of grace, meaning that, in my case, if Pam and I hadn't met, another tenacious inroad of truth would've breached my fortress container, even had I gone the psychopathic route. But the fact is, another alternative did *not* happen in this universe. Pam did.

It's *how* Pam and I did it that makes it possible for me to write the rest of this memoir.

Pam—Like I said, she's beautiful.

Chapter 7

Expectation Objectification Frustration Relation

Oh, you might recall
Now did I act carefully, did I do right?
Or were we meant to be, all of our lives
In love and harmony, all of our lives?
So now, take my hand
Come, hold me closely
As near as you can
Believing all that we could be
And all that we have been
And all that we are
—"You Might Recall"/Genesis

Inherent to how Pam and I made it to this day are also the seeds of relationship demise. Tonics are tight-wire balancing acts over a vat of toxic chemicals.

Happy—and without a clue.

Pam and I certainly had our cyclic patterns of behavior. Some days or years, we cycled in a rut, ever returning to the same level we started on the mountain. In other years, months, days, instants, we got vertigo at our sudden ascent. Sometimes the sheer futility of going nowhere spurs a terrific lift in altitude—the seeds of destruction, ennui, frustration, and despair actually foster ascent. Those times we thought ourselves hitting a peak, we desultorily realized we were back where we started. When we felt our most phone-it-in, pointless, one-foot-in-front-of-the-other drudgery, we rubbed our eyes to see ourselves at a much higher vantage on the upper slopes. Ninety-nine percent of the time, we dovetailed perfectly—loving, parenting, job and career moves that on the surface seemed insane but paid off in ways that exceeded our wildest expectations, believing in and upholding each other, consoling and uplifting each other through disappointment and dark nights of the soul. But for recovering perfectionists like me and Pam, 99 triumphs pale in comparison to the one clash we have, the one failure in which we feel like we've let down each other, ourselves, our kids, and everyone else.

Latent gender dysphoria loosed two bloodhounds on the trail of my fleeing self—anxiety and depression, baying at my heels. I built fortresses and joined tribes to hide from their snapping jaws. But those dogs relentlessly tore down my walls, resulting in a hopelessness that deadened my ability to appreciate the gifts Pam extended to me. Pam despaired of my finding happiness, turning her anguish on herself. I saw myself as her toxin, much in the same way I'd always felt toxic to myself. In my malaise, I lashed out at inconsequential shit, snarling at other drivers on the road, customer service agents on the phone, a baseball or hockey game, my inability to repair something in the house. The baths of serotonin my body summoned to calm these outbursts drained my reserves, funking me out for hours or days. Alarmed at my sheer volume and bombast, Pam couldn't help but intervene. "Well, you cut in front of them."

"Why are you taking their side?" I barked back. When she pointed out the holes in my retorts and rationalizations, I fell into a brooding meant to punish her. Pam, like no other, has the ability to prevent my putting feelings on the shelf. So, deal with them I would have to, even if I couldn't express them in ways other than fearful anger or sullen gloom. For Pam, striving to meet expectations renders her often unable to vocalize negative emotions. To unveil messy feelings is to endanger the chance to delight others.* I come from an Italian family for whom a holiday meal of bellowing at one another about politics, sex, religion, and family dysfunction ends with everyone exhausted and saying, "That was great!" Catharsis is bliss. Pam's family dynamic assigns ugly and loud confrontations to the ninth circle of hell because they signal total failure to deliver on the expectation of harmony and composure. Again, both Pam and I have come a long way up the mountain from these foundational family ruts and actually now complement one another. But the intervening years weren't so kind to either us or our kiddos. It became a semiannual ritual for all of us to have a hollering, screaming, crying, snot-filled adventure that ended with us at iHOP at 3am, some feeling release, others saying "What the hell just happened?"

Confrontation being a death sentence for Pam but catharsis for the yahoo I used to be, our arguments fell into a pattern. I'd get insecure and push Pam to tell me what was wrong, Pam all the time trying to escape the corner of the fortress I hounded her into. Finally, Pam would vent her feelings. I would fire back. Instead of the give-and-take, blow-for-blow I expected, Pam would shut down or cry, leading me to think she was mourning the hopeless, horrible brute I was. Yet, she cried because, once out of her mouth, the ugly emotions ruined any chance at delight. For me, just when stuff was on the table, Pam left the table in despair. Early in our marriage, I'd pursue her, leaving her no space to process. Later, I punished her by brooding. Sadly, in those latter instances, *I* was the one who acted like *she* were too far gone to merit a reply.

These flash points were indicative of a deeper issue that, if unaddressed, would break us.

Something had to give.

---

* For the record, the overwhelming majority of folks *are* delighted by Pam. To me, their delight is not so much the result of her expectation-meeting but because she's a spontaneous and beautiful person. But mansplaining that to her led to the occasional 1-out-of-100 snafus. I'm happy to say that she's ascended up the mountain on this one—a little of which might have to do with my no longer mansplaining.

June 2017—Our last pre-Bethany wedding anniversary.

Chapter 8

Something's Gotta Give

Anger and resentment are first lines of defense when a person feels that she is doing more than her fair share or more than is reciprocated.
The unfairnesses that we intuit and experience but cannot "prove,"
as we are asked to do so often, are more likely to become internalized anger rather than externalized action.
—Soraya Chemaly, *Rage Becomes Her*

Our relationship chimed a chord, mostly in harmony, sometimes in cacophony, that has never since stopped sounding.

It's a severe mercy Pam didn't kill me.

For the next four years after we got engaged—two in which she and I were 24/7 together at UD* and two in which we were 1,800 miles apart while I got my M.A. at Penn State and she completed her Bachelors at UD—we made a courtship that was the proving ground for the worst that wedded life could throw at us. After her graduation, we got married, settling in Dallas. As big UD Catholics are trained to do, we embarked upon rearing little Catholics, having first our son, Atticus, then two years later, our daughter Gertrude, and another two years later, our younger son, Liam. Each was uniquely gifted and suited for the time and place in which they were born and raised. I'd worked at a financial services company in Las Colinas, and two years later, we bought our first home in the bedroom community of Krum, TX, where, in 1993, I was elected Mayor, beating a two-term incumbent, for the non-paying honor of being the chief executive of a not-even-one-light town.

---

* Pam forewent her Rome semester because of little old me, one of many sacrifices she's made through the years.

First apartment, first baby.
Christ, we were babies ourselves! Can you see the '80s all over us?

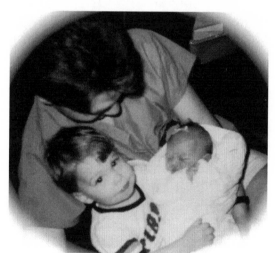

1990: Me, holding Atticus (almost 2) and Gertrude (newborn). Big Catholics breed little Catholics.

We continued in our Catholicism, but it was becoming a strain
on a family with three small children and the nearest Catholic
parish miles away. Living in the real world, outside the UD
bubble, we met people who weren't products of Catholic
academia. Further, because we were taught to be "independent
thinkers," we began to think more independently from Catholic
dogma. Further, we'd been trying to commute 60 miles to our

UD parish, which was making it harder and harder to fulfill the Sunday-Mass obligation. So, we made an effort to join the nearest Catholic parish in Denton, the county seat, ten miles away. Only when we sat down with its priest did we manifest just how far from conservative Catholic sensibilities we'd come. In the midst of our asking Fr. Rob (who initially expressed no compunction at our calling him "Rob") questions about the parish, the discussion veered into the political tenor of the parish, which, in Catholic circles revolves around either abortion or LGBTQIA+ stances. Wow. That escalated quickly, especially when we recognized freedom of reproductive choice as the law of the land. When Pam had prefaced a certain point with "Rob ..." Fr. Rob pounded his fist and yelled, "You shall call me *Father*!"

That ended the discussion. We didn't file for excommunication, but our fervor for all things Catholic, as well as our Mass attendance, fell off after that.

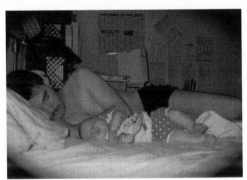

Me and baby Gertie

My responsibilities as Mayor and my job and three kiddos meant a lot going on, which involved a lot of objectification on my part, as there was neither time nor space to feel deeply about the things I was going through. Pam, too, held down her own job. Things often got messy, as they will when two smart and passionate people raise a family of passionately smart kids. Becoming deeply involved in all things Krum, we innocently sent Atti (going on 6) and Gertrude (just turned 4) to Krum First United Methodist Church's week-long Vacation Bible School.†

---

† Liam was just 18 months old, so he rattled around with us while Atti and Gertie learned all sorts of fun songs and did all manner of summer-craft projects.

What was even cooler was that Krum FUMC had a *female* pastor (who made no demands that we call her anything but "Miriam" and with whom we had delightful theological conversations, there being no one else in Krum who had our level of theological interest). Not only did we become fast friends with Miriam, we got active in Krum FUMC. Soon after we started regularly attending, we noticed a kind middle-aged gentleman in a dapper suit sit down in our pew, greeting us. I turned to Pam. "Uh, I think that's Bishop Morris."

Pam surreptitiously looked down the pew. "Are you sure?"

"He looks like the photos of Bishop Morris in the church newsletter and the *UMC Reporter.*"

Pam glanced again. "I think you're right. Do we tell Miriam?"

"Lemme confirm it's him."

I turned to Bishop Morris and said, "By the way, Bishop, it sure is nice to have you in our little church this morning."

He nodded his head, and we exchanged pleasantries in which I raved about Miriam as the second coming of Christ. I then high-tailed it to the church basement where Miriam was prepping.

"Uh, Miriam, the Bishop is sitting in the congregation."

Have you ever seen a meerkat with its eyes popping out? Yeah, Miriam was that meerkat. "What? Are you sure?"

"Yeah. I made a bet with him on today's Cowboys game."

She would've slapped me if she hadn't turned whiter than an altar cloth. "Oh no! My sermon today is on *The Runaway Bunny!*"

"The Runway What?"

"The kids' book, *The RunAway Bunny!* I can't preach that to the Bishop!"

"Miriam, you're a heckuva a preacher. I'm sure the Bishop would appreciate the unique angle of your preaching on *The Runaway Meerk*—I mean—*Runaway Bunny.*"

"Oh, G-d! He'll send me to Greenland FUMC."

"Nonsense, Miriam! His jurisdiction's in Texas, not the Arctic."

As my Mayoral term ran down, I didn't run for reelection. I wanted to spend more time with the kids when I wasn't at my full-time job, and I had a new tribal pursuit—not just United Methodism but *ordained ministry* in the United Methodist Church. As usual, Pam had the idea first. I latched onto it when I saw she was dead serious. *Both* of us could out-tribe the tribe on this one, I realized. Pam's motivations had no tribal inclinations, but, regardless, the two of us made it our calling. Within a year, we'd interviewed with the North Texas Conference Committee on Ordained Ministry and won full-tuition scholarships to Brite Divinity School at TCU.

Boy did we ever belong at Brite! We graduated 1st (Pam) and 2nd (moi) in our class, had several professors as surrogate parents/grandparents for the kiddos, and explored doctorates in Theology. I even revolutionized the Brite style guide on the use of spaces after periods at the end of sentences. Our Hebrew Bible professor had noted in one of my papers that I wasn't inserting what she considered the requisite *two* spaces after a sentence-ending period. From all my corporate work as a managing editor of a training department, I reasoned with her that the advances of the personal computer and adjustable fonts rendered double spaces obsolete. I then showed it to her on the intrawebs' version of the Chicago Manual of Style. (All this evidences the "how-many-angels-can-dance-on-the-head-of-a-pin" concerns of both perfectionist me and top theological minds. You can see how I so fit into this tribe.) "Oh my g-d, Jasper," my Hebrew Bible Prof said at the next faculty meeting. "The Beelers are right. We've been doing it all wrong."

Glad we settled *that.*

As much as I felt in-my-tribe at seminary, I knew without a doubt that I was *not* in my tribe in the local churches for which I was part-time student pastor. It was like Fayettenam revisited, except in the East Texas Piney Woods, which in many ways make Appalachia look like Plato's Academy. I most manifestly *didn't* belong there, which didn't stop me from taking up the challenge with a desperate fervency. The board chair of one little rural church I served made it his mission to eviscerate me because I dared ask for the cord to the copier (rural congregations of fewer than 60 members are *rife* with the theft of copies, and therefore the copier cord must be kept under Fort-Knox surveillance).

In another instance, I'd noticed there were four UMCs within four square miles of each other—the two tiny churches I served and two African-American UMC congregations. I'd heard tell at seminary that Sunday-morning church was the most segregated hour in America. This was East Texas and, apparently, Jesus resurrected only with the permission of Jim Crow. When my two churches held their annual summer revival, I good-naturedly invited the two African-American UMC members and pastor to attend. Not only did they come, but they joined our choir for the revival. Hot damn! Our choir never sounded so good!

A week later, I was invited by the Trustees Committee Chair to visit with him and his wife at their home, where he told me, "I don't like how you're running this church!"

I didn't run shit. I was a student pastor who'd be gone as soon as my seminary tenure ended.

"Really?" I said. "I'm sorry to hear that. Can you give me an idea of what things you aren't liking?"

"Well, I know some may not think it's Christian, but I don't like that you invited *[insert forbidden racial slur here]* to our church."

This one was *much* easier than control of a copier cord. "You're absolutely right. It *isn't* Christian in any way, shape, or form. So be my guest in not letting the door hit your ass on the way out the next time you get your knickers in a knot over who comes to church. Have a good day."

On Pam's front, every new congregation she went to had *never* had a female pastor. A few people literally left the church. One couple even told Pam, "Yes, dear, we think you and your family are wonderful people. But what you're doing is against G-d's will." Again, don't let the door graze your posterior on your trot over to the Southern Baptist congregation next door.

Yet, not only did I not seek out my first post-seminary appointment in an urban setting, *I made it my mission* to be the pastor of and ambassador for tiny rural churches, serving on the Conference and National Small-Church Committees. To whom was I trying to prove something? To the church folks? They didn't care. Methodism is a revolving-door system whereby ministers are assigned by bishops and serve only a certain number of years at any given appointment. "Wait a while," those church members reason. "This one'll be gone soon enough." More significantly, what the hell was I trying to prove to myself? *Hey, Fayettenams everywhere! I survived y'all and gone out into the world and seen the light. I carry it back to you. Now will you accept me?*

People return to toxic and dysfunctional settings. It's why the abused so inexplicably stay with their abusers. In my youth, I'd suffered the rurally and willfully ignorant. Having rammed my head into that brick wall, I revisited the scene to make it right ... without ever asking myself if it could *ever* be anything other than what it is. Even worse, I didn't bother to ask whether *they* wanted (or *needed*) the sunshine I was peddling. Most critically, I never asked myself who *I* was meant to be. Joisting with windmills became a terrific distraction from seeing my true self, as well as the recapitulation of a pattern in which I was fully tenured—objectification. Where would I have been least likely to discover I'm trans? Tiny, rural, stagnant places have to be near the top of the list. That I had a heart for them is beside the point of my having a calling to *know my own heart*.

In my third appointment as a rural church pastor, I was assigned to two congregations whose only reason to be yoked was to afford the salary of a full-time minister. One congregation was a celebration of civil religion, worshipping the flag, the U.S. military, and singing "America the Beautiful" at every chance they got ... and this was the sunnier option. The darker one was an old, moribund congregation in a sparsely populated area. The only thing not dead about it was a small collection of retirees who'd tied up church funds in the infrastructure and the church cemetery, apparently taking only "Let the dead bury the dead" from Jesus and ignoring the "Follow me" part of that scripture.

Just because a group of people is backward thinking in terms of race and other social issues doesn't mean they can't be crafty sons of bitches. This smug little oligarchy had installed as their board chair a personal injury attorney who may have been the unhappiest person I've ever met. One time in a Finance Committee meeting, he declared, "I'm proud to say that never has there been one dissenting vote in a church meeting I've led."

I was nonplussed. Remember, this was "I-spilled-ink-on-Will's-dress" me. I promptly replied, "I also know a body politic that never had a dissenting vote—the Soviet Politburo."

I've seen only one person in my life who turned that shade of apoplectic purple. If I didn't already have a target on my back, that Board Chair and his masters saw to it that I got body-slammed and Kung-Fu kicked every time I turned around. They walked out of meetings, threatened to cut off my salary, begrudged my going to Pennsylvania to lead the funeral service of my dad who died after an eight-year battle with cancer. Church tribes deal death to outsiders, and I was not one of the tribe.

Soon, I saw that I was not one with even myself. Something had given way, and I was in free fall.

East Texas wasn't rural enough for me, so I went on a mission trip to preach in rural Uganda

Chapter 9

Second Gift and Second Dose of Religion

If you have forgiven yourself for being imperfect, you can now do it for everybody else, too. If you have not forgiven yourself, I am afraid you will likely pass on your sadness, absurdity, judgment, and futility to others.
—Richard Rohr

I couldn't sleep because of the gnawing in my guts. I couldn't concentrate. Everything about church filled me with dread. My life bounced like a popcorn kernel on a hot stove top.

I felt worthless, useless, bereft of any and all support. The United Methodist system was just that—a cold, unfeeling system for crowd management that was 8th-grade all over again, except I didn't have even the outlet of tweaking the nose of a ridiculous authority figure. For *I* was that authority figure.

And what had I authored? A thorough dissociation from my own feelings that left me clueless as to who inhabited my skin. I desperately began job hunting, but where to start? I'd been out of the job-hunt game for a decade. I'd tossed my life into the Methodist tribal basket only to become a basket case.

While Pam's congregation had, after a very rough initiation, adjusted to and now grudgingly affirmed her being a female pastor, Pam had about two years earlier experienced her share of abuse and alienation from the sausage-making business called church. Atti, Gertie, and Liam, thankfully, were thriving, but they were heading into their secondary school years, and how could we pay for their college if we bottomed out of ministry? Vocational burn-out was bad enough, but mine had turned into full-fledged general anxiety disorder and depression. Thankfully, a dearheart of a soul and friend referred me to her own therapist, who pinpointed the meds I needed to restore a regular sleep schedule, tamp down panic attacks, and regulate my serotonin levels. But the damage was done. My fortress was shattered, and I sat in its ashes like Job in sackcloth, scraping my wounds with a potsherd.

Therapy and meds brought equilibrium to the church situation, but, for the first time in my life, the fight was gone from me. Previously, I could square the enemy in my sights—and, oddly, it usually turned out to be a woman against whom I lashed out or on whom I pinned the source of my woes—Miss Bordas, Laura, girlfriends who'd dumped me, Lucy, my mom with whom I'd clashed over the intervening years, even Pam when she and I argued. But this time, who was the villainess? This time, I had to collect the feelings I'd refused to feel through a lifetime of shelf curating. Where to begin? The library was wrecked.

No one crisis intervention can enable a person to pick up all the pieces. It's a matter of triage, determining the life-impinging wounds and saving for later attention the less threatening ones. That's what Ann, my therapist, and I began to do. I had to examine my motives in having affiliated with the Methodist tribe. In what did I place my worth? If Pam and I couldn't see ourselves persisting in ministry, what then was calling our hearts? Ann presciently asked me, "What would you do if you had total freedom in your situation right now?"

Without hesitation, I said, "Walk straight into a Catholic church."

Pam was again ahead of me on this. About two years earlier, she felt a hunger for the Catholic Church—where she couldn't possibly occupy a leadership position. Slowly, in the midst of my crisis, I, too, began to return to fundamental forms of prayer that underlie the Catholic imagination—the Liturgy of the Hours, contemplative meditation, and the Rosary.

"But how can we even begin to take steps in that direction?" I asked Pam. "Both our salaries come from the UMC."

"I could teach in a Catholic school," she said.

"And what are we gonna do about housing?" I replied. We lived in the parsonage provided by her UMC congregation and paid no rent or utilities. Hell, we didn't even own the furniture.

"Our family can't fit in the empty parsonage at my churches," I lamented. "And there's no way I'm gonna put myself in 24/7 proximity to that brood of vipers. Atti's 15 going on 16. He's gonna hit college age soon, and we won't have a dime of savings for tuition if we use it all to make this move."

"Then we wait for the right moment," whispered Pam.

That right moment might not come till retirement. I was 40 and Pam 38. Our Texas UMC Conference stretched from Texarkana to the Gulf Coast. We could be appointed to any point in-between, and we'd developed close ties with the Bryan/College Station area, 20 miles away, because our kids, especially Gertie, were heavily involved in community theatre there.

Though the next six months was a stuck-in-a-rut cycle around the mountain, it was a gift that allowed me no pretensions, no wish to cultivate any further the tribe from which I'd been alienated. Our tribe was our family. We did our jobs and made sure our kids were safe, whole, and growing into their best selves. In the meantime, I still wasn't convinced about returning to the Catholic Church. Thank God I couldn't become a priest! I'd had enough of the sausage-making underbelly of ordained ministry. But, increasingly, I felt a tug to the Eucharist and to Mary. I also found ways to devote my talents to things other than the pearls-before-swine proposition of nursing a dysfunctional and unappreciative congregation. We'd homeschooled Atti, Gertie, and Liam through their late elementary and middle-school grades because the local school district was, for me, all too reminiscent of Junior High West, and for Pam, herself an educator, far below our kids' abilities. Connecting with a network of homeschooling families in Bryan/College Station, I used my MA in English to offer home-school co-op courses in composition and literature. We formed a small, tightly knit group of young people Atti's age who thrived on my teaching. Sometimes I'd bring Liam with me, though he wasn't a class member. One day, he declared, "Mom, I'll stay in your Methodist confirmation classes, but when it comes time, I don't want to be confirmed in the UMC."

"Oh," said Pam. "What's brought you to this decision?"

"I've been listening to Dad teach Dante's *Divine Comedy*, and I think the Catholics get it right. I'll become Catholic."

A child shall lead them.

We talked at length with Liam, thinking that, if we took him to Saturday-night Mass, he would get a better feel for things. All three of our little ones had been baptized in the Catholic Church, but, of the three, Liam had had the least exposure to the big R.C., as he was not even two years old when we'd left the Church. We assumed that attending a couple of Masses would wear out his catechumenate hankerings. If he took to it like a fish to water, then at least one of our family would be making proactive strides toward the goal Pam and I felt increasingly drawn to.

Liam loved Mass. What's more, so did we. It's hard for anyone who hasn't spent time in the Church to grasp that, walking back into a Catholic sanctuary, a flood of familiar smells, sights, feelings, and gestures greets you. Unlike the Protestant milieu, Catholic folk don't glom onto you as you grace the threshold. Short of using holy water to down an aspirin, you can walk into a Catholic church and be left to your own devices. The candles and stained glass, the whisper of your clothes against the pews, the Mary and saint statues in the sconces, the lingering smell of incense, the hush and swish of people quietly moving about the sanctuary—who needs a mainline Protestant usher to greet you with a membership form, church bulletin, and invitation to the potluck social afterwards in the fellowship hall? A Catholic sanctuary alone is a feast for the senses.

I was a *tabula rasa* at this point, having had my fortress torn down. Instead of courting a new tribe, I was the Prodigal come home to the Catholic familial embrace. It was the severe mercy of a second gift. The first had been Lucy's, whose name, by no accident, means "light." The second gift was the depression and anxiety I'd gone through at the hands of my congregation. That gift was the chance to start over with myself. What better way to do that than to return to a place, which, in comparison, felt like home? Attending Saturday night Mass smacked of going "under cover," hiding our identity as Protestant ministers, while drinking from a well that quenched our thirst in a way that our UMC careers had ceased to do.

I thought we'd been spinning donuts around the same level of the mountain, when we'd ascended to an upper slope. From that higher perch, we saw we *could* take steps to transition out of the UMC. Not only would we not hurt the development of our kids, we would thereby enhance them. After all, we'd abandoned our previous careers to go into ministry, and Gertie, Atticus, and Liam had thrived with the transition. We would make no move until we'd secured new jobs and a place to live.

In early April 2005, we talked with Fr. Ian, the winsome priest of the parish where we'd taken Liam to Saturday-night Mass. This priestly exchange went markedly better than our previous one. He didn't think we were half-cocked but that our plan was sound, and he knew the local Catholic high school was looking for teachers. He put in a good word for us with the school president and with the Monsignor of its sponsoring parish. A week later, we landed secondary teaching jobs (me in Tech Writing, English, and Latin; Pam in Theology) beginning with the fall semester in August. A week after that, we signed a two-year lease on a four-bedroom house in Bryan the same day we handed in our ministerial credentials to our gape-mouthed UMC District Superintendent. In addition, we secured supplemental jobs (because Catholic school teaching pays for shit) working evenings and weekends in a restaurant that friends of ours owned, me behind the grill. The day after our last Sunday as UMC ministers, Pam, Liam, and I were received back into the Catholic Church, taking our first communion in 11 years.*

As usual, when Pam and I move on something, it happens swiftly—maybe too swiftly for my own good. In the ruins of my old fortress, I started a new one. This time, it would be impregnable. Determined not to leave the Church again due to what I characterized as my lapse in faith, I meant to out-Catholic

---

* We let Atticus and Gertie choose their own paths. For them, the move was not so much a change in churches as one of locales, with easier access to the community theatre company they loved. Atticus came into the Catholic Church a year later, and Gertie 18 months later, though both have since gone their separate ways from Catholicism.

the Vatican. Pam and I went to daily Mass. I said rosaries as I worked the grill that summer, and we both did the Liturgy of the Hours. I devoured Catholic texts I hadn't seen in years, reading apologetics and prepping myself for the classes I'd teach that fall. We enrolled Gertie and Liam at the Catholic school where we taught, Atticus opting to continue homeschooling his final year before he went to college at, you guessed it—UD.

Atticus, in his own UD-Rome-semester posed photo

When school started, we'd awake at 5am, arrive at 7am to

open the school, teach till 3:30pm, then scramble to the restaurant on the other side of town where I worked the grill and Pam managed, both of us till midnight. Then we'd crank it back up the next day, feeling too grateful to notice our fatigue. Besides, the lifestyle energized us, as we not only were immersed in the Catholic spiritual life we'd hungered for but also got to teach it.

Bryan/College Station (BCS), home to Texas A&M University, (TAMU) is almost entirely a university town in what is probably the most conservative area of Texas, an already dyed-in-red state. BCS is the yang to Austin's (home of blood rival UT) isolated-liberal Texas yin. So, in essence, I hadn't shaken my Fayettenam gravitational tendencies—just transferred them to another denomination. In trying to outdo the Pope, I not only didn't chafe at the Church's stances on abortion, LGBTQIA+ issues, and human sexuality but endorsed them with a vigor meant to preempt any new "lapsing." The socio-cultural make-up of the typical family at the school where we taught was as conservative as the backwoods UMC congregations I'd left in my wake. But I was now the paragon, ubermensch, and self-appointed press secretary of the traditionalist camp. My statements in the classroom and social media, as well as my Mass attendance and practice of the sacraments, were immaculate. I had *arrived,* people! Our first year a success, we were entrenched in the school family and mindset, and looked forward to a second year of greater triumphs—one in which we could graduate out of our restaurant jobs to better-paying, less-exhausting side positions and move out of rental housing to a home of our own. But the end of our first year, undetectable to us, boded a coming tsunami that would make my anxiety-riddled run-ins with dysfunctional UMC congregations a comparative April shower.

In the meantime, I took on part-time work as an adjunct faculty at the local community college and with a test-prep firm, teaching GRE, GMAT, LSAT, SAT, and ACT prep. Pam became not only a part-time Youth Minister at the school's parish but also its baptismal and marriage-prep coordinator. Between us, we now had six jobs, Atticus at UD, Gertie in her Senior year, and Liam in eighth grade. We were as deep into the Catholic tribe as we could get. I repeated the pattern I'd blazed in the UMC—infiltrating a group and trying to prove that I was a pillar of the tribal meeting hall … that was about to collapse around my ears.

Spring of 2007, in the last two months of our second year, Pam was the coordinator of the school's academic-competition team that qualified for the state finals. On the overnight trip to Austin that she chaperoned, Pam caught students imbibing liquor they'd smuggled in their suitcases. The school administererd punishments that in the minds of the students' families, marred their senior year. *Church people deal death.* The more backward, recalcitrant, and traditionalist these persons' beliefs are, the more heartless, utilitarian, and vicious they'll be in pursuit of vengeance … because they believe they're righteously doing the will of G-d. A mother of one of the alcohol-sneaking kids leveled with the bishop false accusations against me and Pam, tantamount to live-sacrificing a baby on the school-chapel altar.

As the diocese launched an investigation, we were not allowed to be at the school for the last six weeks of the semester, while Gertie and Liam tried to see through their Senior and 8th-grade years with this cloud hanging over them. We were guilty-until-proven-innocent. I cliff-dove into the depths of Hades, suffering a perpetual anxiety attack as I awaited news of the investigation *and* the closing on our house—not knowing whether we'd be exonerated or homeless. My counselor asked whether I would resign. I'm a fighter, remember? Even when fighting means near self-destruction. But it wasn't *self*-destruction. Pam and I were being attacked by the tribe to which we'd devoted ourselves. In this dire state, I failed to see the deeper issue—that I couldn't keep on joining tribes as a way to affirm myself. Yet, the agony in my guts, brain, and heart forced that truth onto the back burner. My counselor advised me on treatment, plus the name of a lawyer who would take on our case for a minimal charge.

Prostrate with anxiety, I got meds, then called the lawyer's office. The lawyer's secretary recognized our names, for that secretary had been one of the few sympathetic members of the UMC congregation that had plagued me. She pressed Maria, the attorney, to take our case. The universe wasn't out to get me, the first of many evidences to come in the following years to forever secure my retirement from the fortress-building profession.

Maria single-handedly showed me why lawyers are not the scum of civilization as they're often portrayed to be. For every legal team that defends child molesters in the Catholic church, there's a Maria who says, "Cut the crap. I know the case. Are you under any medication that would impact a polygraph?"

"Uh, do antidepressants count?" I asked.

"Shit!" she said. "Is your wife on any meds?"

"No."

"Get her over here in half-an-hour for a polygraph."

Again, Pam made a beyond-belief sacrifice. Despite the wreck that was our lives, she underwent that polygraph test. That night, she was going to the school's choral program that Gertie was headlining and that would immerse Pam into a crowd of the very people who'd accused us. My mom, who'd come down to help us with our move (Mom and I had come a long way in recent years, making up for lost opportunities), said, "The moment I saw Pam shotgun those two jiggers of tequila before she went to the choral program was when I finally got Pam."

Shootin' tequila (Anejo or Reposado, mind you, though, at that time, all we had on hand was run-of-the-mill Cuervo) and takin' names. *That's my Baby!*

After weeks of getting no response from the diocesan investigator as to the status of our case, Maria called him into her office. As she led him down the hall, she snapped back over her shoulder, "The kid and his mom are liars. I have a polygraph." Ten minutes later, the investigator waddled out of the office like a beaten cur. In two weeks, we were exonerated.

I wish I could say that we heartily celebrated, but we were drained. I was numb from the medication and trying to put back all the scattered pieces, even while I taught test prep that summer. Pam somehow continued to lead church-youth. Despite undergoing this trial, we remained faithful to the Church and as traditionally minded as ever. A large part of it was the chastening effect the investigation had on us. What we had done before to ensure that we were stalwart members of the Catholic Club apparently hadn't been enough. Even though the Church espoused teachings that Pam and I had doubts about, our positions as teachers required us to toe the party line. In particular, Pam has always been sympathetic to the LGBTQIA+ cause. She would, as a deliverer of information, convey Church teaching that homosexuals were "disordered." When asked in the classroom her own perspective, she had to reply, "My views are beside the point; this is what the Church teaches."

I, meanwhile, in the classroom, described trans persons as engaging in "self-mutilation." I was wrong then in what I said and hideous for the anguish I caused. But it's telling that the Catholic church launched an investigation into false accusations about encouraging alcohol and tobacco among students but not bat an eyelash at my ignorant and hateful pronouncements on LGBTQIA+ persons—some of whom were students in my very classroom. Little did I know I was on a journey, and the hierarchical church and our dysfunctional diocese, parish, and school were manifestly not.

But first a detour into the mental and heart processes that led me to not only support such a broken organization but to spout hate against what would turn out to be my very self.

Chapter 10

The Sacred Feminine: A Turning Point

The Hero's Journey is ... a Call to Adventure, a slaying of dragons ... a quest to be reunited with the lost feminine within us ...

The Feminine's Journey [is a] call to quiet and stillness, receptivity and patience. While the masculine braves a treacherous world, the feminine ... waits in uncertainty ... Not knowing. Not doing. Just being. And ... Enduring suffering that is sometimes so great and never-ending it seems unendurable. But it is here, in this cocoon, that the feminine will ultimately be reunited with the lost masculine.

She is pinned to a cross in which there is no solution. Her task is to bear the heavy tension. And submit to the eternal injustice that befell her. Until hopefully, maybe, one day... grace comes from deep within and all around, and the cross is reconciled.

... the possibility that it will never end is part of what brings her to her knees. She realizes, finally, she is not in charge here ... She must hand it over to the Great Mother ... who teaches us just how much control we do not have—and how much we truly do.

... The Hero's Journey ... is worshipped as the myth of our time ... the Feminine's way ... does not make for million-dollar blockbusters and best-selling novels ... But ... we will either refuse the call or find ourselves ... unable to move forward. Our ... bodies will protest, and our lives may become impossible ...

When [the masculine within] learns to honor and help the way of the feminine, the resistance melts, the way unfolds, and the union draws nearer.
Leyla Aylin/Midwives of the Soul

I've already mentioned Catholicism's don't-ask/don't-tell policy on the sacred feminine. In Catholic dogma, Mary is a created being, not a goddess. Yet, Mary and other female saints are a minority report on the feminine nature of the Beloved amid patriarchal iconography of the divine as a thunder-fisted, bearded, muscular dude who has more in common with Zeus, Jove, or Thor than with the Beloved Whom Jesus of Nazareth embodied.

Catholic spirituality teems with the sacred feminine. The genius (and terrorism) of the Church through 2,000 years of Western history has been its appropriation of pagan faith elements when it can't wipe out the cultural memory of those faiths (think Christmas trees or the placement of Christ's birth feast on the old Roman Saturnalia). Cue Marian devotion's pagan manifestations of the sacred feminine. The persistence of Marian devotion throughout Church history shows that the sacred feminine is *one with human identity.* After all, half the human race is female. Wouldn't it therefore *have* to be obvious to the church patriarchy that the sacred feminine must be given its due? Whether they see it, they do what I did for 50+ years—deny the feminine to the point of misogyny and wield a masculinity that turns toxically upon itself. Witness the systemic denial concomitant with an all-male priesthood composed of a majority (or plurality) of men who:

- at best, recognize their homosexual identity but willingly live bifurcated lives; or

- at worst (and, sadly, this is more often the case), repress homosexual identity, as well as all human sexuality, and desire to the point that it's not addressed in seminaries or in the active administration of the Church from the tiniest diocese on a Pacific Island all the way to the Vatican.

I'm *not* saying that suppression of the sacred feminine creates a homosexual priesthood. Rather, this centuries-old institution's *modus operandi* is to hide, deny, obfuscate, vilify, and persecute various aspects of gender, sexuality, and sexual identity. That the Church has also done this with the sacred feminine is correlative to what it does to LGBTQIA+ persons.

This repression is a primary reason why Church teaching on gender and sexuality has little or no credibility among American and European laity. Parishioners *know* their priests and bishops are in denial when it comes to sexuality. Church teaching simply doesn't correspond with the lived experience of the people in the pews. As of this writing, 68% of American Catholics believe in trans rights and acceptance. Upwards of 75% agree with same-sex marriage. And more than 90% use some form of artificial contraception. In almost every category, American Catholics are the most progressive demographic group in the United States when it comes to issues of sexuality, human reproduction, and human identity. Conservative Catholics and the hierarchy view such divergence as spawned by Vatican-II reforms. Yet they conveniently ignore that Pope Paul VI's *Humanae Vitae,* the encyclical condemning artificial contraception, was itself an attempt to reign in Vatican-II reforms and was rightly received by Western Catholics as a ham-fisted imposition of authority. The laity's summary rejection of the Church's birth-control ban spawned the trend in which faithful, practicing American and European Catholics continue to ignore Church teachings on sexuality and gender. Nonetheless, for 34 years, in a so-called "reform of the Reform," John Paul II and Benedict XVI appointed conservative Church prelates and promulgated reactionary teachings under the notion that "the laity are just misguided"— even as those same prelates denied and suppressed the horrors of clerical molestation of children.

Priestly sex abuse doesn't happen *because* a critical mass of priests are homosexuals. Being LGBTQIA+ has no connection with pedophilia. But as the Church predicates its organizational life on an all-male priesthood that denies the homosexual identity of clergy *and* suppresses the sacred feminine that has been a constant through 100,000 years of humanity on this planet, it therein creates a haven for secrecy, subterfuge, obfuscation, and blatant lying about elemental human matters—a den of shadows that child-molesting predators find conducive to their hideous activities. Such repression thus becomes a dam of scandal that eventually bursts, leaving human wreckage and loss of faith. So my heart burst. And, like the Church, I still didn't learn.

After Lucy, I went straight to objectification and fortress-building. The same with my failed relationships before I met Pam. Even with Pam it was "learn a little, then hide the rest on a shelf." The dam burst in my tenure in the UMC, then again in my second gallivant through Catholic Wally World. This cycle wouldn't stop of its own accord, nor was any one cataclysmic event or steadfast personal programme of mine able to break it. I had to evolve through meanderings up and down the mountain. Sometimes one step forward, two steps back, sometimes five steps forward, two steps back. I made progress only when I was ready for it.

The last chapter's recounting of the depravities I suffered in the Church doesn't indicate how the Catholic imagination ironically *fostered* my embrace of the sacred feminine and my trans identity. When Lady Gaga says that she learned from Catholic nuns how to be the woman she is today, and conservative Catholics scream in outrage, hers isn't some revolutionary intrigue or communist plot to undermine Church teaching. Female Catholic religious have been nearly the *only* persons in the Church to take the sacred feminine and half the human race as sources of grace, hope, and transformation. Saint Maria Goretti did the same thing for me that those nuns did for Lady Gaga.

In 1902, Maria Goretti was murdered at 11 years of age fighting 19-year-old Alessandro Serenelli's attempted rape. He stabbed her 14 times, and she succumbed on her death-bed a few days later, on July 6.* In prison, Alessandro had a dream of Maria extending to him 14 lilies (a symbol of sexual purity) that he took as her forgiveness for each stab wound. His conversion, his begging forgiveness from Maria's mother, and his testimony in Maria's canonization proceedings played an instrumental role in her 1950 canonization.

Yet, a few things get missed in the hagiography surrounding Maria's death. On her death bed, she was goaded by her priest to forgive Alessandro.† Further, urging a feverish attempted-rape-and-murder victim to forgive her attacker as the primary order of business is both gruesome and sadly indicative of endemic patriarchal abuse. "Oh, you've got 14 vicious stab wounds in your neck and torso, and a raging fever? Though we've no pain-killers, and antibiotics are unheard of in our era, let's predicate your deathbed absolution on whether you forgive your attacker." Now

---

*Interestingly, the month/day of my dad's birthday.
† Such hagiography ignores the power dynamic of patriarchy and poverty that put her into Alessandro's clutches and Alessandro himself into an I-get-what-I-want-or-I-kill-you mindset.

that's sensitive pastoral care. Next, many have used her rebuffing Alessandro's attack to victim-shame rape survivors who could not fend off their assailants with the accusatory "Why didn't you fight back?" Finally, her canonization was a cause celeb for a Catholic purity cult that was in full-throttle in the '40s and '50s.

I either missed or subsumed all of that in my personal purity cult. Mary and other female saints seemed far above my lapsed-convert/revert status. Maria Goretti was, for me, a humble, approachable, and inspiring model of faith and purity of intention. I envisioned myself as a knight in her heavenly train while she served as a maiden in Mary's entourage. I say none of that patronizingly, for it was, at that time, the primary way I accessed the sacred feminine in my emotional and spiritual life. Leaving the UMC and becoming a Catholic school-teacher, I rebuilt my fortress in the service of a masculinity that lived out the gender-binary-imposed role of man and father to provide a home to live in and our kids' college education. Maria Goretti was a refuge for me. I adored her unsullied piety, femininity, and capacity of heart that had eluded me through the years. The dude who made girls cry at bus stops could now, like Alessandro, find a new lease on life, via the back door of heaven cracked open by a heroic Italian peasant girl. This, in turn, whet my devotion to the Virgin Mary. I'd bought a handmade prie-dieu and an icon of Mary holding the infant Jesus. In our move from the lease property to our new house, amid the worst throes of the diocesan investigation, I found that the icon had been scratched, as if with claw marks, across the visages of Mary and Jesus. I hung that icon at eye-level above the prie-dieu, and, in the single worst agony of my life, even more torturous that my crying in a darkened bedroom after my mom had told me she was leaving, in the most vicious pains of my depression and anxiety as to whether we'd keep our home and jobs, I knelt, shuddered, and wept, looking straight into the steadfast, scratched-through eyes of Mary, saying to the Beloved, "I love you so much, I love you so much."

At the time, I hurt so intensely that I'd no idea why I wasn't cursing the Beloved for what I was going through. To whom was I professing my love? The Beloved? Mary?

Or ... *myself?*

It was all these and more. I saw myself at the depths, the farthest down I could go, fortress-ruins mocking me, my heart raw and scored, weeping tears of blood. And instead of wretchedness, I saw what the Beloved saw.

Me. With no pretension left.

Me. At my wits end.

Me. Finally feeling the rawness of emotions I'd stored away to protect myself.

Staring back at me was the steady mien of the Beloved. The ultimate feminine that no number of claws could slice into anything but recognition. She stared back at me and knew me.

And I began to know myself.

Mary and my soul. Scarred, but the more loving for it.

Chapter 11

From "Not My Story" to No More Tribes

As we grow in wisdom, we realize that everything belongs, and everything can be received.
We see that life and death are not opposites.
They do not cancel one another out; neither do goodness and badness.
A radical, almost nonsensical "okayness" characterizes the mature believer, which is why
they are often called "holy fools." These wise ones do not have to deny, dismiss, defy, or
ignore reality anymore. What is, is gradually okay (which does not mean you do not work
for justice and truth, but this must be accompanied by a primal yes!).
What is, is still the greatest of teachers.
At the bottom of all reality is always a deep abiding goodness,
or what Merton called "the hidden wholeness."
—Richard Rohr

I thought that being faithful was about becoming someone other than who I was, in other
words, and it was not until this project failed that I began to wonder if my human wholeness
might be more useful to G-d than my exhausting goodness.
—Barbara Brown Taylor

The investigation was not the last abuse the Church and our dysfunctional diocese wreaked on us. In the years between the investigation and our eventually saying "No more!" to the Catholic church, we were lied to by priests, railroaded by various school administrators, and shadowed by the diocese.

Though we thrived as teachers and our students loved us (and we, them), we learned our limits. Pam found a job that allowed her to resign from the school after seven years there, and my burgeoning test-prep work became full-time, enabling me to resign from the school. Both these departures were different from our previous tribe-leavings. We weren't refugees in flight. Rather, our beliefs were growing and changing. One of Pam's favorite *Star Wars* quotes is Princess Leia's sage warning to Tarkin: "The more you tighten your grip, Tarkin, the more star systems will slip through your fingers." As the Church trebled its assault on LGBTQIA+ persons, Pam found it hard to go to Mass in the extremely conservative parishes in Bryan/College Station. While I was still teaching at the school, a student rightly challenged me on my own rigid stance on LGBTQIA+ rights, then, two years later, another student confided in me her own coming out.

"Mr. Beeler," she blurted out after the other students had left class. "I'm a lesbian!"

Rather than being taken aback, I heard myself say to her, "Okay. So, what's next?" The conversation took off from there.

A few days later, she talked in admiration of a male upperclassman, leading me to whisper, "But shouldn't what you told me the other day stop you from being wowed by him?"

She winked. "It doesn't stop me thinking his sister is *fine!*"

When had I joined the lesbian student gossip club?

As Pam's advocacy got to the point that she was battling on social media with conservative Catholics' objecting to her stances, I wondered where this was all going. We'd always had LGBTQIA+ friends. I was never phobic about my gay roomies in college or any other LGBTQIA+ friends or colleagues. In my later tenure at the school and after it, I led a parallel existence— adhering to Church teaching inside my head, while our best and dearest friends were a living refutation of that teaching. Despite all my objectification, flesh-and-blood persons in my book *always* trumped "-isms." I came to an uneasy (and thankfully short-lived) middle-ground in which I told Pam, "I know you support LGBTQIA+ rights, but I'm not because it's not my story."

Zero steps forward, two steps back. How many emotions and truths had I put on the shelf, saying to myself, "Those are not my story," when they most manifestly were?

Pam got a full-time job with the test-prep company I worked for, which had long been LGBTQIA+ friendly. Years before the U.S. Supreme Court's Obergefell ruling that legalized same-sex marriage, one of my colleagues mentioned her wife during an online meeting like it was the most natural thing in the world (which it is). At first, her passing statement jarred me, until I

realized the inflexibility of my mental constructs. I was
transitioning from living in my head to living in the world as it
was given to me.

This journey was aided by my joining a group of third-order
Carmelites, the lay branch of an order of contemplative nuns and
priests. Our local group was pitifully small but laid-back. I'd
grown wary of tribes, which was just as well, given that the
Carmelite discernment process takes from three to ten years. I
took things off the Carmelite shelf and tried them on for size,
finding a connection with female Carmelite contemplative giants,
Teresa d'Avila, Blessed Elizabeth of the Trinity, and Therese of
Lisieux that resonates to this day. For Therese especially, true
contemplation is grounded in our living out the everyday
circumstances of our existence, however humble. Through
Therese's manifestation of the sacred feminine, I grew less
inclined to build a fortress. This contemplative work, in turn,
dismantled my black-and-white thinking. I began to relish the gray
areas between what I'd fixed in my mind and what I encountered
in actual living. Instead of container-building, I engineered a
bridge between head and heart. Things my head had once insisted
were "not my story," my heart said, "Now, there-there. You just
categorize the shelves while I sweep out this room for our guest."

I was that guest, exploring rooms in my heart I'd never seen,
sitting down in them, taking a meal. Under these auspices, I had
my dream of washing my face to reveal a woman in the mirror,
sojourning in my heart with my feminine self at a time when my
head simply couldn't feature it.

I didn't end up committing to the Carmelites, though my stay
with them helped open the highway between my heart and head,
making the two one. A big test of this came when my position as
a Faculty Manager in the test-prep company became so stressful
that it impacted my health. All the symptoms that had previously
plagued me in my attempts to identify myself with a role and a
group reared their ugly heads. But this time, instead of
objectifying my feelings and grinding on till I crashed, I listened
to my body, mind, and heart, and took proactive steps to remedy
the situation. When I pushed back and asked to teach full-time

instead of managing, the company affirmed my discernment, enabling me to experience years of even greater job satisfaction. I joyfully discovered I could constructively defy my tribe and negotiate the terms of my stay without abdicating my identity.

I found a similar liberation in heeding what my heart had always told me about the sacred feminine, feminism, and LGBTQIA+ rights—these were indeed stories worth shouting to the rooftops, even if I still didn't see them as my personal narrative. Besides, how was it anybody's right to dictate what consenting adults did in their own bedrooms? Saying "Not my story" to people who for centuries have been crushed by patriarchal cis-het culture leaves those stories to be told in isolation, if at all, or hijacked by those who hate and objectify any who don't fit the status quo. Ugly behaviors of church tribes showed me what I'd been doing to myself for years—establishing my identity on the basis of who was "in" my group and who was "out," who was worthy and who was not. Tribes are not about the growth and nurture of individuals but about maintaining the tribe. My self-worth as a tribe member was therein derived from how ruthlessly I reinforced tribal integrity—insidiously, by the degree to which I forced myself to mirror the tribe. If I'd done that perfectly, I would have lost my very self. When such loss of identity happens *en masse,* we call it what it is—a cult.*

People beyond my tribally reinforced container were, by their very difference, a testament to something other than what the tribe said I must be—a competing vision of selfhood that, if adopted, could explode the tribe. Thus, we hear from evangelical and Catholic religious cults that the LGBTQIA+ "agenda" threatens the "traditional family," or that not being able to discriminate against LGBTQIA+ persons destroys religious freedom. The animus behind such posturing is that their tribe wields a hegemony of their preference and benefit. They thus

---

*Please don't confuse my epiphany about tribes with the natural human need to belong. We are not islands unto ourselves but derive healthy and necessary meaning from association with other people. Those connections are made possible by recognizing ourselves as worthy of association with others and vice versa. Cultic groups are fueled by alienation and self-loathing.

fear and hate a differing model as an attack on their privilege.†
When the loss of the tribal agenda is one and the same as
preserving our own identity, we then fear the loss of tribal
integrity as the loss of our very selves.

I didn't ask myself until later, *"Why a tribe in the first place?"* Did
I not have an identity before I joined the tribe? If I did, what was
so horrible about me that I needed to conform to a tribe, that I
needed to be anything but myself? I'd for too long seen myself in
terms of what I wasn't, those things I thought I had to be in
order to be accepted, loved, not abandoned: a man in the image
of my dad, a faithful son, a good student, Catholic, a minister, a
teacher, a husband, a father. None of these were the "me" that I
brought to these roles. They were the living out of an expectation
that I should have had the freedom to try on for size. But I hadn't
believed I had such agency, and I'd lived most of my life assuming
I brought nothing to these roles that were prisons. Yet, I'd no idea
what was locked inside the cell. Nor any clue who was the "me"
who kept setting the lock and throwing away the key?

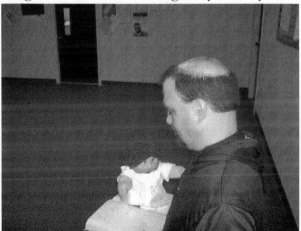

Why, yes, I tonsured myself to win a Catholic-school Saint's Day contest. Talk about conforming to
the tribe! (And that is a Cabbage-Patch Kid. I was trying to be St. Anthony of Padua, and, as I
noted before, the '80s have apparently left their mark on my genome.)

---

†The process is known as "mimesis," as defined by philosopher, Rene Girard. James Allison
offers a brilliant application of mimetic theory in Christian circles in his *Faith Beyond Resentment*.

Chapter 12

The January Itch

You're so gorgeous I'll do anything
I'll kiss you from your feet to where your head begins
You're so perfect you're so right as rain
You make me
Make me, make me, make me hungry again
Everything you do is irresistible
Everything you do is simply kissable
Why can't I be you?
I'll run around in circles 'til I run out of breath
I'll eat you all up
Or I'll just hug you to death
You're so wonderful
Too good to be true
You make me, make me, make me, make me hungry for you
The Cure/"Why Can't I Be You?"

Luther is credited with saying that the drunk man who falls off one side of the horse is bound to fall off the other side. So it was with me. Where I once cerebralized everything to the exclusion of my heart, I now unleashed my heart, irrespective of any caution offered by my mind.

Pam hadn't been exaggerating when she'd asked, *"Why does this happen around this time—the last two Januaries, and now this year?"* The Richard-Dreyfuss character's obsession with the Devil's Tower butte in *Close Encounters of the Third Kind* approximates what happened in the Januaries of 2016 and 2017 when I gave reign to feelings I hadn't explored my entire life. January had always been a slow work period. Forced all those decades into being a closeted librarian, Bethany made her voice heard now that I'd ceased tribe-joining and fortress-building. Yet I kept garbling the message.

It's a severe mercy Bethany didn't kill me.

In January 2016, I became obsessed with the possibility that every man had an unexplored feminine side worth submitting to. It was a feverish fascination I couldn't rationally explain to myself or Pam. At the time, I thought it was so novel that that there was no real-world way for me to live it. I could just feel it, as if that were enough. Being trans never occurred to me, even though, 18 months earlier, I'd applauded Caitlyn Jenner's coming out. I see now that I was finally letting myself explore what I'd objectified for decades. As such, I was totally unfamiliar with that wing of my emotional library. This was the first time I let myself be under the sway of the feminine. The rush of feeling it brought was a return to early puberty when I'd felt the novelty and power of first-time desire. Spinning itself out, that first obsession ended up feeling like, *a la* Shakespeare's Sonnet 129, an "expense of spirit in a waste of shame." When its grip left me, I cast it aside as a mere infatuation. For once, though, I didn't castigate myself for having such feelings or for having explored them. Even though I quickly abandoned it, I was merciful to myself in doing so, as if to say, "Whatever it is I'm looking for, I don't regret having chased it, except for the confusion it caused Pam."

The biggest lesson I gained was Pam's sage summation of it. "Babe, this 'feminine self every man has' actually amounts to your not being a dick. The 'feminine' things you're talking about aren't some radical new way of life but rather a world in which dudes aren't being dicks to women. A guy shouldn't need any grand realization to treat women like human beings."

She nailed it. Someone like me who, despite my egalitarian sensibilities, had been immersed in a male-dominant upbringing, would see as "novel" and "revolutionary" the renunciation of patriarchal dominance. Pam wasn't saying I'd always been a dick to her (though, admittedly, at times I was) but that my expression of the feminine self was long-time in coming and perhaps never coming in many men. What had been the history of patriarchal culture but males treating women as property?*

Gee, that was fun. Why not try a more intense version of it in

---

*When our world treats women as equal, female empowerment will *not* be patriarchy in a dress but the partnership model of equalitarian cultural that thrived in the Paleolithic and Neolithic eras, to the fall of the Minoan civilization (the last remaining partnership culture) in 1500 BCE.

January 2017? Great idea!

What drew me was, again, the opportunity to plunge my entire self into the realm of the feminine. In comparison, a declaration of being trans might've been easier to deal with than the seeming two-persons-in-one-body possession I underwent. At that point, the idea of being trans was thoroughly "not my story." Thus, my internet searches were as subjective and confirmation-biased as any point-of-view that I was mentally, emotionally, physically, and spiritually not ready to see. So, my searches—and the eyes that perused those searches—never alighted on anything of trans ilk. Furthermore, given that I'd blazed my life's trail as a man, I never saw the feminine as a path that actually existed for me. I could play at it, but no more. I could adopt, internally, feminine feelings, but I still had to be a dude. I could get in touch with my china pattern, all the time using the wedding Wedgwood for skeet-shooting. That I thought this an integrated way to live bespeaks the fervor and irrationality with which these feelings hit me. Pam stood her ground that she wasn't down with it. Yet, she also had the compassion to let me explore it. I cannot fully appreciate what it cost her in terms of peace of mind.

But this round, as well, was destined to fade. I wrote it off as another tempest of feeling. Despite this and the previous January's itch, I learned more about myself. With this second dead-end, I exhausted my backlog of feelings previously banished to the closets of my soul, mind, and heart. Clearing out that emotional detritus via this trial-and-error granted me a heart-head balance. I'd broken through two false walls in my fortress. The next breakthrough would be to something real, not a mirage. I left January 2017 having put away childish things and mid-life crises for good. It was time for real living.

As Emerson noted, "When half-gods go, the gods arrive."

Chapter 13

Interlude: Keepers of Secrets

There were no formerly heroic times, and there was no formerly pure generation.
There is no one here but us chickens, and so it has always been: A people busy and
powerful, knowledgeable, ambivalent, important, fearful, and self-aware; a people who
scheme, promote, deceive, and conquer; who pray for their loved ones, and long to flee misery
and skip death. It is a weakening and discoloring idea, that rustic people knew God
personally once upon a time—or even knew selflessness or courage or literature—but that it
is too late for us. In fact, the absolute is available to everyone in every age. There never was
a more holy age than ours, and never a less.
—Annie Dillard

And it was morning
And I found myself mourning
For a childhood that I thought had disappeared
I looked out the window
And I saw a magpie in the rainbow, the rain had gone
I'm not alone, I turned to the mirror
I saw you, the child, that once loved
The child before they broke his heart
Our heart, the heart that I believed was lost

Hey you, surprised? More than surprised
To find the answers to the questions
Were always in your own eyes
—Fish/"Childhood's End?"

Through the years, my relationship with my mom and dad was rocky. Retiring from his corporate job of 35 years to become a local pastor in the UMC, my dad didn't at first take well to my becoming Catholic. Previous to that, he'd bowed out of transporting me to college in Texas (that one fell to my mom and Bill) and, like my Mom, didn't attend my graduation from UD. It was clear that he devoted his attention to Laura and my half-brother, Jason. Dutifully objectifying my feelings about that, I gave him a pass because, after all, this was *Dad*. He visited me, Pam, and the kids several times. On occasion, he volunteered glimpses of the past. My dad's youthful nickname had been "Dink." We'd learned from my mom that "Dink" was short for "Dink the Dickie Dunker," for his proclivities at playing the field with women. *This* corresponded with my youthful experience of his divorcee playah status with beautiful young women. So, when the kids were down for a nap, Pam asked him on one of those visits, "Otis, where did the nickname, 'Dink,' come from?"

"Oh, my friends called me that because I had an old dink of a car," answered Dad.

"Really?" said Pam. "Norma told us that it was short for 'Dink the Dickie Dunker.'"

Me and Dad on my wedding day.
Damn, I couldn't help but love and admire that guy.

My dad got a twinkle in his eye, accompanied by a shit-eating grin. Any time he made a joke that he wanted all to notice, he'd end it with a "Mmmmmm" till somebody laughed. His only response to Pam's revelation was a very long, "Mmmmmmmm."

Later during that visit when we could get him to talk about his and my mom's meeting, dating, and marriage, he'd revealed that Mom had had an affair in the early years of their marriage, before

Brian was born. This was shocking news to me, seeing as how I'd never been told anything about Mom and Dad's hidden married life—not before or after they'd divorced. I was 35 years old at this point. How could I not have been told? Further, in talking about my mom, Dad intimated she'd been sexually abused by her own father, who'd paid for my final semester of undergrad when my mom and dad refused to. "Your mom said to me one time that Pap-Pap had snuck into her bed one night when she was a kid and said, 'You're going to do what your mother won't.'"

My dad was never a malicious soul, and had his grievances with Mom after their split. But he'd never gone so far as making up something horrific about Mom's childhood. Nor was there any continuity in the conversation such that he'd had a reason to fabricate her childhood sexual abuse. As I learned through the years, Dad was a secret-keeper. While he divulged compromising instances of Mom's past, he never once admitted the remotest inkling of his infidelities during his marriage with Mom or his youthful dickie-dunking status. Brian and I held him in golden status—thus no revelations of clay feet. Once he got religion and married Laura, the crypt door was slammed shut by her on his playah proclivities. Then, given his local-pastor status, religion again did a thorough job of denying reality.

Dad began an eight-year battle with the lung cancer that was to eventually take his life. Though he'd never smoked, he'd grown up in the steel-heavy borough of Clairton, PA and had founded the high school's baseball team, playing its games atop a slag heap under a mill-belching carcinogenic sky. He went into remission for a short time after chemo and radiation, but the next time it returned, it metastasized from his lungs to the rest of his body. He died in his bed on September 23, 2003. I was barely 40. A few days later, I did his funeral in front of a church filled with people of all races and colors. Dad's charm and charisma led the entire community to vest him with golden status. He was a good man. But a man, at that, like every other man, with clay feet. I felt robbed of something elemental in that he couldn't show me his ceramic sneakers.

The way I found out about my dad was from an even more

intrepid secret-keeper—Mom—who carried out more than one abandonment of me.

When Pam was bed-ridden for 11 days in the hospital with IBS and lost 60 pounds, my mom, of her own accord, flew down to Texas to help me as I worked my full-time job and took care of Atti (then two-and-a-half) and Gertie (still an infant and still not sleeping through the night). Mom's first evening there, I woke to hear Gertie crying and went to help my mom with her. When I saw that Mom was holding Gertie in a way that I knew was only compounding the kiddo's fussiness, I tried to show Mom a better way to cradle Gertie. Mom plunked Gertie into my arms and said she was getting on a plane home, which she then did. Years later, the story in my mom's mind morphed into her having gotten the flu or a kidney stone and had to fly home.

Another time, Mom and I were arguing over the phone, and I made a point about Dad, to which Mom replied, "Oh, your Dad! I could tell you things about—" and halted. "Never mind."

One June, Pam, the kids, and I were driving from Texas to Fayettenam to vacation with Mom and Bill, when, mid-trip, Mom phoned to say she didn't want to have us and hung up. Two weeks later, she called, asking, "What happened to you and me?"

Other times, Mom did the most random kindnesses. She'd send us money out of nowhere for a home repair or to help us enjoy a vacation. When Bill died, she gave me his SUV. When she halted her own driving, she gave her car to Liam. Later in her life, we'd call her once a week, and she praised Pam and me on how we'd raised the kids to adulthood. She made special effort to prepare me and Brian for her death, ten years before the event, making sure her will was in order, pre-paying her cremation and burial arrangements, leaving an insurance policy and 401K for us to share, and telling us multiple times and in multiple ways she loved us. Those were the years when, out of the blue, she'd un-keep a secret she'd hidden for years at no little cost to herself ... and at a cost to me.

She loved to regale me and Pam with stories about my childhood, from her calling me "Beth Ann" in the womb to my wisdom about leaving dinosaurs alone to an instance in which, while carrying a load of laundry, she tripped on a toy truck I'd left on the stairs and plummeted down the steps, only to have me run up shouting, "You broke-ah da truck!" (I'm told that, as a toddler, I spoke with an Italian accent.)

In the decade before her death, she'd unburden herself in a way that said, "This is hard to hear, but you should know this before I die." In 2013, nearly 30 years after the fact, my mom, out of the blue, tearfully apologized over the phone for not coming to my graduation. In those later years, she, I, and Pam grew closer. Part of it was my voluntary retirement from my tribes and my getting in touch with suppressed emotions and memories. Part of it was her giving me what I call the third gift. She didn't tell everything, didn't admit to every failing. But the gift was that she told me enough ... which helped give me permission to be me.

In fall 2014, she paid my fare for an Amtrak train from Texas to Pennsylvania to see her. She could've sprung for cheaper airfare, but she wanted me to have a vacation, and there was an Amtrak stop in Connellsville, a short walk from her senior-living apartment in which she spent her last years. As we ran errands around Fayettenam on that visit, I talked about how rough it had been for me to grow up there.

"We knew you'd get bullied," she said. "It was always a fine line between stepping in and letting you handle it. You were strong and stood up to it. You had a lot of strength and bravery that other people didn't have. You still do."

I was floored but masked it in front of her. Strong? *I* was *strong?* "Why the hell didn't you tell me that back then?" I wanted to holler. And I should have, adding, "Do you know what that could've meant to me when I was at my lowest, thinking I was weak, cowardly, hateful, and worthless?"

But I didn't say that because her words shocked me. Here I was, 51 years old, never having known that, at one of the most miserable, self-hating times in my life, when I made objectification a high art, I was actually *strong* and *brave.* For years, I thought that, at best, I'd merely survived. Now here we drove through Fayettenam, the scene of the crime, and she tells me I was the hero of story.

I began to regard myself differently. Following her revelation, less and less did I need to man-up. I didn't have to *act* like I was brave and strong because I've *always been* brave and strong. Her words gave me a lens through which I reassessed my history. I became kinder and more merciful to myself, and, in turn, was able to do the same for other people. I was becoming a wounded healer, and it showed in the work I did with students and my life-coaching clients. I was an advocate for the oppressed, taking on stories without checking whether they were my story, too.

For years, I'd told Pam that, when I grew up, I aspired to be like her—brave, beautiful, compassionate, and joyful.

I was beginning to grow into that aspiration.

One Sunday, as I was in the garage, all-grain homebrewing (whaddya want from me? I had a massive man-beard, smoked a long-stem pipe, and wore a kickass cowboy hat—*of course* I homebrewed in 100° Texas heat), I called my mom. We laughed over an incident that had occurred in kindergarten when my teacher, Laura, had called Mom for a parent-teacher meeting.

"Laura was livid," Mom said. "This was her first year of teaching, fresh out of college, you know. Laura proceeded to tell me that, the day before, a little girl in your class had crawled under a desk and wouldn't come out, no matter what Laura said. At this point, honey, Laura stood up straight and described in scandalous terms what you did. '"Well, Mrs. Beeler,' she said. 'Your son strode up and said, "Hey, Suzie, get the hell out from under there!"' Honey, it was like Laura was expecting me to break down mortified, but all I could do was laugh!"

"You *laughed,* Mom?"

"Right in her face, honey! I couldn't help it! But honey, it doesn't end there. Laura rose up in all her dignity and said, 'I suppose he learned that language at home!' I laughed again and said, 'Yeah, you're probably right!'"

Then my mom, in the more vulnerable way she'd been sharing with me in her later years, a sharing that, in turn, led me to share with her, said, "Laura wouldn't talk to me after that. I think she was disappointed that your dad hadn't been the one to come meet with her. She was always eager to see him."

I paused, as the tumblers clicked in my feeble little brain. "Mom," I swallowed. "Are you saying Dad and Laura had something going on even when I was in kindergarten?"

It was her turn to pause. "Well, I couldn't be sure, but, at the time, your dad was, well … she had an eye for him."

"Mom, are you saying Dad had other affairs while you two were married?"

Again, she paused. "… yes, your Dad was like that. It was a problem we had."

This time I *did* ask the question that burned in my mind. "Mom, why didn't you tell me this way back when you two split up? Or even when I was in college?"

"Honey, I'd never do anything to spoil your Dad in yours and Brian's minds. He was your father. You boys looked up to him. I just … kept it to myself. I'm a big girl."

After that call, despite her never having told me at the breakfast table *why* she and Dad were having problems, and despite her not telling me in college when it would have explained why I had such a fucked-up family, I was grateful. Grateful that she'd told me when I was 52 years old. Grateful that she was a secret-keeper even at the cost of smearing her image in the eyes of her children. Grateful that that dysfunction had led me to never be a secret-keeper with my own children.

Mom had a stroke in late November 2017 and lingered until she died on January 27, 2018. When I was in Pennsylvania at her bedside, I knew it was time to shave off my beard, despite giving Pam no warning. Mom had always hated the beard, and, truth to tell, Pam had previously urged me to trim it. It had to go sometime, and that sometime would be a shock for Pam no matter when. Maybe it was a Rubicon that, once crossed, signaled to Pam (and myself) that I wouldn't be going back.

My journey was only beginning.

Me, Mom, and Brian in 1987. Mom was beautiful.
I helped her realize that before she died.

Chapter 14

Of Bunny Trails and Men

Liam (11) and I in Uganda, Summer 2004.
This is who he wants me to be. I still am me. He disagrees.

Fast forward to the moment when I told Liam I was trans. I'd already revealed it to Atticus and Gertie. But Pam had warned me, and I already knew, that Liam would take it the hardest.

Liam was our third child—y'know, the one for whom you throw out the training manual because, hell, all the mistakes you made with the previous two didn't warp them too much. Pam remembers a time when I was at work and she was arms deep in something and couldn't break away. Gertie hollers, "EWWW! Oh, Mom, it's so *gross!*"

"What's going on?" yells Pam from the living room.

"Liam's in the *toilet!*"

Pam pauses. "Is he in head-first or butt-first?"

"He's sitting *inside* it and playing in the water!"

"I'll get there when I can," replies Pam.

We called Liam the Valium Baby. He was a month overdue, making Pam feel like a cross between a walrus and Jupiter. Born in early December, he brought a Christmas peace to our household. We still have videos of Gertie and Atticus holding Liam, like a mini nativity, peace radiating from the scene, Christmas music softly playing in the background. Liam slept and Liam ate and Liam shit. And we watched him with fascinated delight.

After that, he wasn't quiet, but he had an uncanny ability to assess a situation and his surroundings, then adapt himself to the scene. He did it seamlessly with his brother and sister, becoming a buffer between the two of them. Nine months after Liam's birth, when Atti went to his first day of kindergarten, Gertie was adrift, as Atti had been the measuring stick for all her achievements—taking cues from him, comparing herself to him, then taking on challenges he wouldn't or would master at a later age, to prove her mettle. When Liam hit age one, he filled the vacuum of Atti's going to school by becoming Gerti's living doll, such that, until my transition, I could say that Liam had been in drag more times than I ever had been!

Liam (middle), age 7.
I wasn't kidding when I said that Gertie made him her doll.

He was the winsome goofball who, in eighth grade, introduced himself to others by saying, "Hi! Liam Beeler, Class Clown." His ninth-grade English teacher was analyzing Wilde's *The Importance of Being Earnest,* saying that the source of all humor is incongruity. Liam blurted out "That's just like *Animal House!* You know—the part where Bluto eats the golf ball in the soup!"

For his college graduation party in his slum of an apartment, he and his three roommates engineered a residual-alcohol suicide-punch party in which they and their guests painted themselves Smurf-blue and held olive-oil wrestling competitions. The class valedictorian broke his wrist during the shenanigans, which my son thought was a fair trade for the night's celebration.

But he is so much more than that. As spontaneous and hilarious as he can be, I've never met anyone with a super ego like his—motivated, directed by the highest ideals, settling for nothing but wholeness and truth, even when that means sacrifice. Liam also inherited his paternal grandfather's charisma and Pam's good looks. All three of our kids posed their unique gifts and challenges. Of the three, Liam had the most hair-trigger temper, and, as he grew, the most black-and-white way of seeing things.

His decision to be Catholic has never wavered, even when we, his parents, whom he in part led back to the Church, left its confining grasp. His super-ego would lead him to slam-bang decisions in tandem with his ability to see them through with panache and commitment.

Raising him was sometimes like dealing with my dad—his humor, boisterousness, and charm put all my man-up tendencies into full-throttle. In fact, my dad nicknamed him "Mazeroski" for Liam's vigor in playing second base in Little League—and my dad had been at Game 7 of the 1960 World Series when Bill Mazeroski hit the greatest home run in baseball history to topple the Yanks. Thus, when in Liam's company, I was more liable to press Pam's buttons and engage in ribald banter. Liam loved baseball like I loved baseball. He latched onto sports fantasies like I had as a child. He played bass guitar and guitar like Brian had, and loved the same music I had and in the same way. I was determined that he would get the boyhood I'd never enjoyed because of the collapse of my parents' marriage. So, with him in the house, I strove to be all the things a dad should be. And Liam regularly pointed out my parenting and behavioral inconsistencies as only a know-everything adolescent can.

When he went to UD (you thought he'd go anywhere else?), he charmed professors in a way I hadn't, and I was so proud. He was loved and looked up to at UD, as I might've been, if I'd been like my dad. His UD career seemed effortless, yet Pam and I saw how hard he worked at that very intense school, and we supported him in every way. Liam launch-padded from the UD experience into the Catholic adulthood to which he aspired, marrying his UD sweetheart, Sharon, (a love relationship that had started as a Rome-mance, no less!) and raising a family, with Elanor, their daughter, born when he was just 23. The little family bought their first home when he was 24. He even succeeded and thrived in Catholicism as I hadn't, becoming a development director for an entire diocese, earning the respect and confidence of the bishop, priests, and diocesan lay leadership.

Despite my jaundiced experience with the Church, I was proud of the course he was setting for himself, his family, and his career, even as Pam and I were pulling away from Catholic influences. Empty-nesting, we finished renovations on the house we'd owned for 10 years and sold it for a profit, enabling us to move into a studio loft in historic downtown Bryan. Go downtown, and, in the sidewalk in front of the restored Queen Theatre, you can see a brick we donated with the name of our first grandchild engraved on it. We found our niche downtown, a slightly left-leaning pocket in the otherwise ultra-conservative Brazos Valley. We had a core cadre of friends we'd made at our favorite watering hole, Rev, a dirt bar with a fantastic beer selection, the best punk-act venue east of Austin, and people who were more real and welcoming than any church denizens we'd mixed with. We also got our first of many tats downtown, thanks to the amazing handiwork of Cliff, Scott, and Audrey at Arsenal Tattoo. You either just get one tattoo in an innocuous spot on your body to say you've done it, or you get one, then another, then one in an FML (fuck-my-life) spot that means you'll never again land a respectable job … which reveals that you're addicted. Pam and I now have more than a dozen tats each and are scouting out future ones. We were living our best life, in an environment in which I had the space to discover I'm trans.

On-cam in GoogleHangouts, I came out to Gertie, who, with our son-in-law and three fur-baby dogs, lives in Boston. Although she didn't see it coming, her immediate response to my identifying as trans was unreserved enthusiasm and support, summed up by her saying, "You do you, Boo!" For her, the main benefit was that she could call me "Bethany" instead of "Dad," as Gertie, since age 12, had been calling her mom "Pam." Atticus expressed no objection to my coming out, saying, "Let me process this." Which he then did after sharing with his dearest friends, then came to Bryan from Dallas a few weeks later to visit and said, "Yeah, nothing's changed—you're still you." Gertie and Atticus, second only to Pam, have been my strongest, most loving, and steadfast supporters, for whom I am more than grateful. They are a lifeline.

Then the hammer dropped. Not everybody thought we were living our best lives, especially if "best life" involved being trans. It's a confession of my obliviousness that I had so identified Liam with the integrity of our family unit that I missed the extent to which he and Sharon were individuating themselves from the trajectory of the rest of the family. Pam, Atticus, Gertrude, and I had all moved out of the Catholic fold in our own ways. For our various reasons, we'd realized that Catholicism wasn't true to who we are. Liam continues as of this writing to see it as his core, having taken so well to UD, Catholicism, and manhood because that's where he's at home. Given our drift away from the Church, he increasingly *wasn't* at-home with us.

I wanted to tell him in-person, but seeing him, Sharon, and Elanor meant arranging a visit. Sharon was in her first trimester with our second granddaughter, Hannah, so just showing up at their door wouldn't be considerate or practical. I called to let him know I wanted to come up. At this point, Pam had not yet had her epiphany and wasn't ready to join me in visiting them. Right away, then, Liam knew something was up.

"Why isn't Mom coming?"

"I want to talk 1:1. Just a day trip. I'm not staying over."

"Are you and Mom getting divorced?"

"What? No! What I want to talk about needs to be face-to-face." At this point, I wasn't 24/7 *en femme*, nor would I visit Liam that way. I hadn't started HRT or come out publicly. Given my family history, secret-keeping was out-of-the-question. My transition would be *with* my kids' knowledge because close family is part of the trans journey. That so many trans folk are rejected by family is one reason why many trans persons publicly tell their stories, to lend support to those cut off from loved ones.

"Dad, this is stressing me. What is it you have to tell me?"

"Liam, trust me—this has to be done in-person."

"Dad, I won't sleep between now and when you would come up. Can't you just tell me over the phone?"

Here, I made a mistake, though I realize that, no matter how I'd done it, he would have had the same reaction. "Well," I sighed, "You may have noticed on FB that I'd shaved my beard."

"We'd seen that and wondered about it. You loved the beard."

"I did, but a lot of things have been changing for me, and it's more than the beard being shaved off. This is something that's been with me all my life, but I'd never been able to recognize it until recently. You see, I'm transgender."

Silence on the other end of the line. "How is Mom with this?"

"She's wrestling with it, I won't lie. I don't speak for her. You can talk with her yourself about it. But I've been up-front with her every step of the way, and I'm doing everything possible to give her the space to deal with this."

"But Dad, you were always the one to talk about self-sacrificial love. Can't you sacrifice this because you love Mom and don't want to put her through this?"

"Liam, I *have* been sacrificing all my life, and I can't do it anymore. She has a right to have whatever response she has, even if that means I lose her. But how can I be real with her if I'm not real to myself?"

Liam paused. "Dad, this is just like the reckless decisions your parents made that caused such hurt. You're stronger than they were. You need to rise above this."

I didn't defend myself because I knew this news had him reeling. "Liam, it seems sudden to you, but it's something I've lived with all my life but never knew or understood. It's caused my anxiety, depression, my joining one tribe after another, and my anger. I've been wrestling with this realization for months, and now I finally feel at home with myself."

"Are you taking hormones and getting surgery?"

This felt like an interrogation. "Liam, I won't know those things till after I've lived with this. But given how I feel right now, yes, I would do HRT if it's viable for me."

"Dad, please, don't do anything permanent. You're a man; that's a reality. Your biology is against this. Science is against this. Let me talk with Sharon about your visiting. In the meantime, pray about this. Think about what you're doing to yourself and Mom. Don't give in to this selfishness. Fight the good fight."

He called Pam after that and tried to triangulate her. Yes, he was worried about her, but attacking me was a sure way to get Pam to think and speak sympathetically about my situation—and a lot more accurately than Liam could because Pam had been there with me *and* with herself through this, even if, at that point, she hadn't resolved what she would do. Liam questioned what, to him, was the abruptness of it, and Pam told him that it was something deeper than that. To be fair, given my life story, I know Liam saw this as my going down another bunny trail. He tried to say that I was doing this because of my right ear's sudden (and, as it now turns out, permanent) hearing-loss four months previous, and because of my mom's recent death. Pam assured him that neither was the case. When Liam offered their home as a refuge for Pam to "leave this unhealthy lifestyle," Pam had to explain that she had already taken time away from me, staying three weeks with close friends. She was back, now, and coming to a decision.

Two days later, Liam sent a text message saying that a visit wasn't practical or necessary. After that, radio silence.

Until I came out publicly.

Chapter 15

Half-Gods Gone

Cling with life to the maid;
But when the surprise,
First vague shadow of surmise
Flits across her bosom young,
Of a joy apart from thee,
Free be she, fancy-free;
Nor thou detain her vesture's hem,
Nor the palest rose she flung
From her summer diadem.

Though thou loved her as thyself,
As a self of purer clay,
Though her parting dims the day,
Stealing grace from all alive;
Heartily know,
When half-gods go,
The gods arrive.
—Ralph Waldo Emerson/"Give All to Love"

1/12/2018

I went to see my therapist today. I hadn't related all the details of
what I'm experiencing before she interrupted, conflated my
situation totally with my and Pam's sex life, then recommended
our seeking out a sex therapist. *SIGH.* That's not the issue.

1/15/2018—MLK Day

A genuine act of faith is … an ongoing dialogue of divine
disclosure and human response—an ever deeper divine disclosure
and an ever deeper human response—just like any human love
affair. People who are incapable of vulnerability thus cannot get
very far on the journey of faith … Simply put, God reveals
God's self to us through what unfolds as our life, along with every

visible thing around us. These ordinary revelations must be respected and deeply listened to.—Richard Rohr

I find myself in the midst of dialogue and disclosure … with Bethany … that's also a dialogue and disclosure with the Beloved. Bethany delights in me and thereby gives me the beloved self-image I've never allowed myself.

Yesterday, for the first time since I was a teen, I crossdressed. And I *LOVED IT!* I shaved my legs (which was a surprisingly pleasant experience). I never looked at my body in the way that shaving my legs made me see it. Yes, I've shaven my face for many years (long before the beard), but it was always a "let's get this thing done because it's the only way I can be presentable at my job, etc." I know that women might also feel the same way about shaving their legs and armpits, and I realize that, if I continue shaving my legs, I may come to see it the same way—that I'm glorifying something that ain't all that glorious. I get it. It still was a cool process. When I put on the tights, it felt absolutely *GLORIOUS!!* It's strange that opaque, control-top tights would give me such a feeling of liberation, but they did! I felt amazing!

I was, in my own small way, receiving the face of the "other"—Bethany—and empathizing with it … to find that she's always empathized with me. I said to myself, "I'm not going back."

1/16/2018

Yesterday morning/afternoon, after I'd written the previous entry, I was tied up with the whole disability-leave/doctor's-notes bullshit. I finally had to wrangle the staff to give me a brief appointment with the ENT. He agreed to give me a note, similar to the last one his office had sent to the office overseeing disability leave, which was all I needed in the first place. As I waited in the hall for a staff member to type the note and for the ENT to sign it, I quelled my swirling thoughts by imagining myself in the eye of a storm. While the crazy feelings and doings sloshed about me, I just stepped into the calm center. Frazzling myself with "What-ifs" and OMGs! used to trigger anxiety.

Today, I saw myself as a source of peace. Events will swirl about me. Let them. I will be peace.

That's what this trans discernment is for me. Unlike my other life transitions and crises, this doesn't swirl me in confusion. I'm at home with it. Battling this peace is my familiar, doubting, perfectionist self who wants a refuge beyond criticism and regret. But what does it hurt to try this road?

<u>1/16/18</u>—Pam's Additional Thoughts

<u>Pam</u>: So, I know you're not purposefully trying to do anything to hurt me. The same is true the other way around. So, Imma try to say where I'm at in ways that don't sound hurtful. I'm biding my time until at least mid-February. I don't mean that in a way that dismisses you, your feelings, or what you're going through. But it's a necessarily Pam-centric position.

<u>Me</u>: Waiting it out is best. Just know that, in the meantime, I'm going to be doing me. When I crossdress here, I'll do so when you're at Rev. Send me a text from there when you're wanting to return if you don't want to see me *en femme*.

That being said, if I live this out beyond mid-February, I'll want to do more than crossdress when you're not around. I'm exploring things, none of which involve irrevocable decisions. I learn from each experience whether this road is for me.

<u>Pam</u>: For now, the Rev solution works. We can revisit in March. For the past two years, I've turned myself into a knot every January. Each time you were "discovering things about yourself." You spent time, money, and effort on the new-found you. And each time you became a shadow of the you I thought I knew … a shadow that made me feel awkward and uncomfortable at best. Then, come mid-February, it was done, and I felt stupid for getting bent-out-of-shape. If it's real this time, it'll be there in March … and if it isn't, I have neither the emotional reserves nor

the desire to get weirded out again. You often say that you know you're difficult to live with. It's never true the way you mean it, but it is true that you sometimes wear me out. This go-around, I'm already worn as far as I can be. So, I'm replenishing in case I need an extra supply of that indomitable Pam-spirit come March.

Me: Yes, I have learned a lot about myself from those previous ventures, though I regret the pain they caused you. If they were shadows, it's because they were shadow-boxing. This time, something substantial casts the shadow on which I'm throwing light. If I hide it, then I really *am* a shadow of what I'm supposed to be. This time is different. This feels at home. The proof will be in the living. And, right now, despite the mysterious loss of hearing in my right ear, I feel like I'm living well. My balance has returned. With it, a balance inside me, too.

This is me; we can live with it or we can live like it's not up for discussion till we decide it's real. But at what date does one of us pronounce it as a done deal? Did we do that as parents? Did we do that with our marriage? Events unfolded, and we've taken them as they come.

Pam: I hear what you're saying, and the best I can do is tell you I'm not there. I don't like it. It creeps me out. I don't want to resent you, dislike you, or feel embarrassed by you. If this is real, it's gonna take me time to get to a place where I can accept it. We said, "for better or worse," so I'm in it for the long haul, but that means part of the haul is quiet for a while so I can get my head around something I don't like/want.

Me: I know I wear you out. You wear me out, too. And I love you for that. Because the wearing out regenerates me like a caterpillar in a chrysalis. I'm ever emerging because of you, and I hope I do the same for you.

Pam: Well, you do sometimes, but this situation is the exhausted kind of wearing out. I'm trying to tell you in as nice a way I can that I'm at a very worn-out place. It's in everyone's best interest that I not get pushed beyond that. For realz.

1/18/2018

> *Jesus undid the mask of disguise and revealed that our true loyalty was seldom really to God, but to power, money, and group belonging. (In fact, religion is often the easiest place to hide from God.)*
> —Richard Rohr

> *Partially, I think what I wanted was to belong. If being female—to others, at any rate—seemed to include self-doubt, insecurity, and anorexia, then some part of me felt, Okay, well, let's do all that, then.*

> *Later, when I tried to let some of this go, there were some who saw me as "less female"—like when I ordered the barbecued baby back ribs for lunch instead of a salad and a diet soda. Why shouldn't a woman eat real food for lunch, I wondered, instead of the pretend kind?*

> *I realized, as Jimmy Durante used to say, that "them's the conditions what prevails," but it didn't sit well with me. There were times when it was as if I were trying to prove I was truly female by oppressing myself.*
> —Jennifer Finney Boylan, S*he's Not There*

Yesterday, I read the Jennifer Finney Boylan excerpt to Pam, and we talked about the need to "belong" and how it directed our lives. As Methodist clergy and, later, Catholic teachers, we tried to belong in the kinds of groups in which we most couldn't belong.

This is a danger in my current feelings about wanting to be a woman. I do indeed have a deeper female self. But what does that mean? Is this another attempt to belong to an impossible group? Or is this an evolution, a revelation, an unfolding, a blossoming?

For years, I've played a man so thoroughly that I convinced even myself—so well that my female self was unknown. I don't want my female self to be another vain attempt to belong. I already belong, as I am, with the Beloved. If I'm a woman, it's to better embrace what I already have—the Beloved and my beloved self.

1/19/2018

> *The face of human suffering is the same whether it belongs to a Hindu, Buddhist, Muslim, Jew, or Christian, to a person who's gay or straight, who's a believer or an unbeliever. If we don't see this, it's because we haven't risked looking into the suffering face of another.*—Richard Rohr

The suffering face of the other I haven't looked into until now is Bethany. She gazes back, reflecting the suffering I cast onto her.

1/21/2018

> *we sat in a darkened movie theater watching* The Lord of the Rings *… Frodo reunites with old Bilbo Baggins in Rivendell and Bilbo tries to get Frodo to show him the Ring. For a moment Bilbo seems transformed into Gollum. Then he diminishes, and a look of exhaustion and horror comes over him.*
>
> *"I understand now," Bilbo says. "Put it away! I am sorry. Sorry you have come in for this burden, sorry about everything."*
> —Jennifer Finney Boylan, *She's Not There*

There's another suffering person in this equation—Pam. She and I talked yesterday, and there were tears. What precipitated it was my coming home with skirts, shoes, and dresses I'd bought from Goodwill and Payless. I was excited and showed them to Pam. What an insensitive, dumbass I am. Pam is in no way on-board with this, and I can understand that—and it's causing her intense pain. She says that she married a man and that she is in this for the long haul. But that still doesn't stop the pain she feels, and that devastates me. I don't argue her feelings; I listen and tell her she has every right to feel awful.

Her pain, in turn, makes me question what I'm experiencing. Is this just a fantasy that I'm indulging at the price of the one I love? I could be throwing away the best thing I've ever had—this lifetime with an incredible woman, not to mention her peace of heart—for something that seems ephemeral in comparison.

1/22/2018

I'm still wondering where this might lead. When I first became aware a month ago, I was certain that I was not going to look into HRT and SRS. But the more I embrace my female self, the more she rings true to me. Repressed for decades from my conscious thought, she's having a heyday right now. Shopping to try on shoes and clothing ought to surely throw a wet blanket on my ardor. But those activities have awakened an even greater longing to commune with Bethany. I don't get to define the end-journey. I'm still learning about myself. (And what I'm learning is that, every time I pass those new shoes, I get a stomach-dropping, doe-eyed feeling.) After reading the WPATH standards of care for transitioning, I'm now saying, "Why can't I?"

The power of these feelings, combined with Pam's pain, has me questioning myself and my motives. So, I pause to detect rose-colored glasses. It's hard to put the brakes on those feelings, and I don't believe that my reason need be separate from my feelings. An integrated self is, after all, the goal here. So much of me has *not* been integrated … for decades.

1/23-25/2018

Pam and I drove to PA to be with my dying mom, which has given me time to further reflect. I think of Brian and how he would not get any of this. Right now, he and I have had too much to attend to. How I am as a man, a son, a brother, a husband these past few days illustrates the many blessings my male self gives me. That's just it: *my female self's emergence doesn't eradicate my years of donning a male persona. My female self has shaped, and in turn, is informed by all I've done in playing the role of a man.*

I shaved off my beard, and it didn't freak me out (I used to have nightmares in which it was shaved off). It did hugely disappoint Pam, as I'd told her I wouldn't jump the gun on that. It's another step in trying on this female self to see whether it matches what's going on inside me. Yet, the sheer power of feeling, in which I knowingly break a promise, makes me question this whole thing.

1/30/2018

Pam's waiting to see if my discernment lasts. Along with that, she's frightened and dismayed by my buying clothes, painting my toenails, shaving my beard. My words here can't approximate what she's feeling. But writing what I imagine to be her experience helps me better grasp the bomb I'm dropping on her. I said this today on the trans discussion forum I'm in:

> *Let's ponder with our spouses/SOs, and let it inspire some compassion and mercy; think from their perspective what these changes are doing to them. They married what they perceived to be men. Our being men also fulfills a lot in their own identities as wives and women. For years, they fulfilled that role with much sacrifice and with much reward—and with much expectation of us.*

> *Our discerning whether we're trans is a tidal-wave they never saw coming. How bewildering that is. While we've lived inside our closets for some time (wittingly or unwittingly), it's like, as Helen Boyd notes, they've suddenly been locked in our closet with us. What's exciting to us excruciates them, making them question all that they know about us, themselves, their judgment, our judgment, and what the future holds for them.*

Carrying on is what I'm doing. I don't broach the subject conversationally unless Pam invites it. Respect her space. Clearly communicate. Realize we live in the same dwelling, and that she feels intense pain and uncertainty. She needs to know that I'm still me amid this transition.

1/31/2018

Last night, Pam had a meltdown. She's horribly and painfully torn. Though she's passionate for LGBTQIA+ causes and wants to support my journey, she's incredibly hurt and fearful that she's lost the man she married. Moreover, she's terrified that one-day revealing this to our grown children would crush them.

I can definitely see that a trust has been broken between us. It can be regained, but it'll take work. She feels I've been pursuing this in a total disregard of her. I feel that I'd tried and tried to talk with her about it, to have her be part of what's been happening to me and that she shut me down, not believing I would follow through on the exploration. Now that I am, she sees how serious I am. She wants her husband back—yet I can't go back. I know we can get through this. We're going to have dinner and talk tonight. We need to navigate our respective expectations and to understand that happiness is not necessarily getting what we want but rather embracing what we already have.

2/4/2018

Much has developed in the past five days:

1. We've agreed that I'll dress and present as female without her present.

2. I told her my female self isn't going away, that I'd be lying if I promised to never think about it again.

3. She asked, if I had the choice today to undergo HRT, would I? I said yes, but that I don't yet know enough about myself to say clearly that I will/won't transition one day.

4. Even after this, Pam said she loves and supports me; it's more than I could have hoped for, given the agony I know this causes her. She is amazing.

As I go down this road, the more real it becomes. What might've been just an imagining weeks ago is bearing fruit in my body. I now feel a physical pang in the pit of my stomach—a good pang, not one of anxiety. I am changing. I am Bethany.

I broke down in tears yesterday. It was the first time that I allowed myself to be the Bethany I've always been. She's been so long tamped down, beaten, hidden, lied about, denied to my very consciousness. Bringing out Bethany ushered a wild sense of freedom. I felt myself curling up as a woman, weeping as a woman, being a woman. Being myself. Being Bethany. Being *me*.

I've sent emails to two gender therapists in Bryan. If either of these doesn't work out, I'll drive to Austin or Houston to establish a solid patient-therapist relationship. I've so many questions to explore:

- Do I just need to crossdress occasionally to live out my female self? Or …

- Do I need to present as a woman 24/7?

- If presenting full-time, does transitioning via hormones and surgery become my route?

Part-time crossdressing doesn't feel like the answer. I need to be who I am, *as I am, all the time.* Whether that's the path to wholeness or is a by-product of novelty and passing moods, I'll discover in the living.

I didn't seek this out because I was conscious of dysphoria, but rather an unresolved pursuit of what I then considered to be anxiety and depression. Meds and therapy helped my depression/anxiety but were only symptom-treatment. An undefined displacement was the source of my anxiety and depression—of feeling I never belonged, of always playing a role good enough to fool everyone but not enough to keep at bay the feeling that I'd slip up and be caught as flawed, broken, miscast. Bethany stood in the back-corner of my heart and cleared her throat. She's speaking now. Correction: *I* am speaking now.

2/5/2018

Last night, Pam called me Bethany. It was liberating to hear my name. I cried because I'm tender right now, in body and soul.

2/6/2018

I came out to Vaughn today, and it was a very healing exchange. I said I felt like I was ruining Pam's life. He said I need not to be so hard on myself. I'm being honest with Pam. The pain she's experiencing, though not separate from what I've broached, is nonetheless her reaction. I am not willingly inflicting pain on her.

Vaughn also confirmed that letting Pam process is the best course right now. He talked about Pam and I being clear with ourselves about "the price of admission," as in what we're willing to accept to stay in relationship. The problem for me is knowing what exactly I've got here. How am I to know what the ultimate price will be if I don't know what this thing truly is?

I'm sticking with what I know: Bethany is ascendant. Right now, I'm in a comfortable and pretty black-lace skirt and white-w/-black-polka-dots blouse, nude control-top panty hose, and cute black pumps. *I LOVE THIS!!*

What, then, do I know right now? I love having my outside match the Bethany inside. I'm learning. I'm going to play with and enjoy this, as well as feel the anxiety and loss-of-control that this fluid situation brings. I'm dancing.

2/8/2018—Pam's Birthday

> *Many people early in their transition, and some later too, worry that they're being selfish by exploring their gender identity. They're not. Your gender identity is you. If it's taken you a long time to discover it, then that's not your fault. Society puts enormous pressure on people to not identify as transgender; it takes a lot of courage to finally explore your gender identity. That's to be celebrated and commended."*—Mia Violet, "Yes, You're 'Trans Enough' to Be Transgender"

It is so liberating to hear this! I've been thinking that maybe I'm just indulging in a crazy fantasy at the cost of everything. But I'm not. I know I am a woman. I will keep on reading, will go to therapy, and be open to evidence to the contrary. But right now, I know in my heart … *I am Bethany.*

2/9/2018

Things aren't so good today. Pam is leaving for three weeks to be in an environment that doesn't immerse her in my transition. I'm probably going to lose her, and that feels impossible to conceive. Yet, I feel attacked (as Pam must feel). We're trapped in an either/or situation that's neither real nor fair. It doesn't have to be this way. I feel like I'm being given an ultimatum, which is no context in which to discern something clearly. To be fair to Pam, I also understand she must feel the same. She can't see clearly when she's choked in the smoke of living with me while I'm giving every sign that I'm eager to transition.

But that's the point: I'm in the grip of some powerful gender dysphoria—which is no ambient in which to see anything clearly. That's why I'm not committing to anything. Yet, in the meantime, Pam dangles, as do I. She's made clear that she cannot live with me as a woman. She married a man.

I wouldn't willingly compromise our life together on a whim. That's why I'm trying to find out whether this *is* a whim. Yet, I know it's not. But how far am I willing to go with this?

Why does embracing my female self have to be to the exclusion of our life-giving relationship? It doesn't have to be an either/or. It should be a path to something beyond the either/or. To greater life. Why is this price so great right now? Why does it have to kill the playfulness of this journey? I can't see beyond this smoke.

So, I wait for it to clear. And dwell in powerlessness—something I'm not good at. Which might be the point. This powerlessness is somehow part of the playfulness. But I can't feel that right now. So, I ache. And so does Pam.

Bring on the separation. Either we'll live this through, or we'll emerge anew as something different.

It's a helluva pressurized chrysalis.

2/11/2018

Turns out that powerlessness *is* a form of playfulness. Powerlessness is indeed a starting point for love and abundance.

Pam is not leaving me. She's gonna visit friends and get some away time through the beginning of March. This is a liminal period. Threshold crossing is rarely graceful; most of us don't do it well. This is our way of being merciful to ourselves and each other. All relationships undergo the change/development of one or both spouses. This is one of them.

Since Pam and I talked about this and agreed to her taking this time off, a load has been lifted off our shoulders. She leaves tomorrow but is even now helping me size bras online. She is amazing me and humbling me with her sacrifice and compassion. I will miss her these next three weeks, but it gives me time to go 24/7 *en femme* and to pursue therapy and a support group.

2/14/2018—Valentine's Day

Another few days in which much has occurred. Monday night (2/12), I went to the local Transgender Support Group and met four other individuals (all MtF). It was nice to talk the language, to meet others who are further down-the-road than I am.

Earlier on Monday, Pam sent a message to four of our dear friends (with my blessing), talking about the situation. I would have rather come out to them myself, but I understand Pam's need to do this. Here's the conversation:

> PAM's MESSAGE—
> I wanted to let you know about some stuff so you didn't feel sideswiped if you hear it from someone else. After the shit show that was the end of 2017 and January of 2018, I am taking a little break from living at

the loft with Beeler. This week I'm staying with a friend in BCS, next two weeks in Louisiana with friends.

If/when people ask why, we are saying that after three months of being together in a 900-sq ft loft 24/7 during Beeler's illness that led to hearing loss, we just needed to have some breathing room, and since I had to go to Louisiana to see a show anyway, this seemed like the perfect time.

That answer is not an untruth … but neither is it complete. Right after Christmas, Beeler started identifying as gender-fluid but now is exploring a transgender identity. Beeler has an appointment scheduled with a therapist who specializes in LGBTQIA+ and gender issues.

The Pam Beeler whom we all know and love would normally encourage such exploration for anyone who was struggling with gender identity issues. Hell, she would even provide them with resources, help with clothing decisions, and take them to the bathroom with her so they would be safe.

The Pam Beeler who is married to a trans-exploring person, however, is flipping her shit in about 56 different ways. I need time and space to process and decide what is a fair and appropriate reaction given both my views regarding gender issues in general and the fact that never in a million years would I have called this, nor am I sure that I want to spend my retirement years being a living example of something that in theory I'm all for. I can't do that processing fairly or rationally if I am confronted daily with the situation.

Likewise, Beeler needs time and space to live with feelings and process wants and needs without every time doing something that hurts me deeply.

So, a little three-week respite from each other seemed a good idea. I'm not telling y'all this to make things awkward or to violate Beeler's privacy or even to ask you for help or advice (though, of course, you're welcome to give it), but rather so that you know a pretty serious thing that's going on with a member of the fam and, to be truthful, so you can avoid making me feel like shit if I show up at Rev one night in my car by saying something like, "Geezus Pam, was the walk from two buildings down too much for you?"

Beeler would have wanted to tell y'all face-to-face but knows that this will be jarring, and wanted to give you time to process too. And, because you're our family, I didn't want there to be secrets between us.

BETHANY'S RESPONSE—
Sooooo, Pam let me know she wuz gonna send this. She's spot-on about a number of things:

1) Never in a million years did I see this coming.

2) I wanted to tell each of you in-person, but I know this is difficult for Pam, and we both need our posse.

3) As a couple, we are *not* going away.

1ST RESPONDENT—My first reaction is that I love you both. My second reaction is that I love you each individually. Past that, I support taking time to take care of yourself. And the rest, I'm going to take a few to chew on it. But I'm here.

PAM—Love you … individually and collectively!

BETHANY—So, don't worry about pronouns or names at this point. I'm not going public till I know what this thing is. Here's what I do know:

1) I've lifelong suffered from anxiety and depression—not even knowing that I did so until I was in my 40s. (Hell, I just thought I was an asshole.)

2) Meds have helped, but not all the way. I didn't know

what was eating Gilbert Grape, to put it in Johnny-Depp terms.

3) I spent all my years in furious activity—working since I was 15, going overdrive in school/college/grad school/workforce, marrying the most incredible woman in the world and being blessed with three kids that I hope I didn't fuck up too much.

4) None of the above was conducive to understanding what was eating at me. I was living as best I knew how.

5) I've repressed until very recently feeling like I wasn't all here as a man. I literally stumbled onto the idea that I might be something different than the person I was always desperately trying to be. It's taken a toll.

That's about the best I can do right now to make sense of this to y'all who know me. If you feel like I've been deceiving you, join the club. I feel like I've been deceiving *me*. Please know   I've always been as real to y'all as I know how. I just discovered, recently, that there was more hiding behind that beard than I thought.

Pam didn't bargain for this, and it's horribly unfair to her. Neither of us knew any of this throughout all the years of our wonderful union.

For the time being, I'm learning what all this means and being honest with Pam to the point that, yes, I want her to take some time off from me. Don't worry about bringing it up with me. Just know that we're keeping this to just y'all, our tight circle. I love you.

2ND RESPONDENT—Please know I love you both very much.

1ST RESPONDENT—Shoulder no guilt from me. I don't feel any level of hoodwinked or bamboozled. I'm still learning about me, so you're still learning about me. You get the same room from me.

3RD RESPONDENT—I didn't feel it as urgent that I reply since Pam looped me in on the situation already. Just wanted to say that I love you all.

Later that night at Rev, Pam outed me to two other friends, which miffed me because she hasn't the right to tell my story without my permission. Yet, I know that she was just trying to cope. I got over myself.

Yesterday, my breast forms, pocket-bra, and make-up came in. I wore my new chest the whole rest of the day, even though I was still in my man clothes. It felt *EXTRAORDINARY!!!*

Today, I've felt intense pangs to be a woman. I think about women, and, yes, I want to kiss them, be with them—my heterosexuality is 100% and that won't ever change—but I want to be with them *AS* a woman. It sends a tremor racing from my throat, through my heart, to my toes.

2/17/2018

Pam and I have been meeting off and on; she's grieving, and the prospect of the loss of us is testing everything about our relationship. Though that's terribly painful and scary, I know in my heart that our struggles are ultimately a good thing.

Last night, I held her while she cried. For her, it's simply not fair: she feels like she worked hard through this marriage, to raise a family, to strive through careers, to come to a point at which both us could get to know each other better in the empty nest and live out some dreams she's had. We're certainly getting to know each other better! I'm learning things about myself, and, in turn, Pam is having to learn things about me that are a challenge. Though it feels to both of us like our dreams are lost, and an abyss yawns before us with no dream that includes the both of us, what if the dreams remain … but in a form we can't imagine?

Bethany is me. I am a woman, and I love it. I am at home. The gnawing anxiety that has always been my life is gone now that I know my true self. I know what I seek: *what kind of woman am I going to be?* I'm forgiving and loving what, for 54 years, seemed to be imperfect, unworthy, excluded, separate, and wrong. Bethany is no longer an enemy or a lurker. *She is me.*

<u>2/21/2018</u>

On Sunday night, I did my own make-up for the first time. A bit gruesome, but I'm happy with it.

Yesterday, I saw Cindy for gender therapy and talked about the voice of self-recrimination and doubt that hounds me through this, the same voice that's been with me all my life, that second-guesses me. The voice that wants to please others so I don't get abandoned. The voice that tells me to be a chameleon. The voice of my self-hatred.

Cindy told me to engage the voice, here in my journal. Talk with it—expose its ruthless questioning, recrimination, and castigation. Here goes:

> <u>The Voice</u>: Why are you doing this to yourself? Why are you putting yourself through this? Do you have a gender-bender version of Munchausen's syndrome? Are you so suggestible that you just fall into the novelty of wanting to become a woman? Look at what you're doing to Pam and your marriage and your life! She's going to leave you, you know. Then you'll be in ruins.

> <u>Me</u>: Hello, Voice. You don't usually expect answers to your questions, 'cuz they're all rhetorical. But I'll treat them here like they're truly inquiries.

> I'm not doing anything to myself. *Bethany* is happening to me. She is me. I am her. And I love her. I love *me.* Do you think I would upend my life on a lark? That I would find all the struggle and change this involves as something enticing? Nope. It's happening because I've

opened a door to air and light and hope—and *ME*—into rooms of my heart that I haven't explored.

Say I do have gender Munchausen's. Okay, then, I'm sick. But what does knowing *that* profit me? What treatment do you suggest other than the one you've applied through the years—tying down Bethany, muzzling her, raping her, shutting her up into a closet so impenetrable that I didn't even know it was there? That's no cure—it's obliteration.

<u>The Voice</u>: Maybe it's a good thing to obliterate! For the sake of Pam and your happiness and wholeness.

<u>Me</u>: You've never been about my happiness and wholeness but about fending off regret, confrontation, and suffering. And at what price? Play a role and never know myself? You've spent my life gaslighting me into being the manly, righteous person I thought I had to be in order to be loved. Bethany blasts away the container you've built—a container not to protect me, but to hide me from myself.

I'm not hiding anymore.

Love—Bethany

<u>2/24/2018</u>

Made dinner tonight for Walker, and we had an uplifting conversation about my trans status. I told him about the Voice, and he imparted some wisdom his mother gave him when he was especially self-loathing about being gay: "Most people have a superiority complex when it comes to seeing the worst in themselves." The Voice in a nutshell!

<u>3/4/2018</u>—

SO MUCH HAS HAPPENED IN THE LAST WEEK!

- Monday, 2/25—Went to Sarah's salon, and she made me up *BEAUTIFULLY!* I was so enthralled with how I looked that I shopped *en femme* (to buy some jewelry chain to elongate a couple of chokers and bracelets) and nobody batted an eyelash. Then, while I was waiting at Newk's for a to-go salad, I went to the *LADIES* room. The sky didn't fall, and no one demanded my birth certificate.

  That night, I was going to stay home *en femme* while Pam went to Trivia at Rev. But she msgd. me that she needed me down at Rev to help our team win, even if I was *en femme*. So, I went … *and made official my coming out!* Everyone was welcoming (if a little shocked!). Here's a pic of us.

- Tuesday, 2/26—I met online with my Austin group therapist. She was wonderful and wanted me to be part of her group therapy on every other Tuesday in Austin. My first meeting with the group is Tuesday, March 13. Then, I again went to Rev *en femme!*

- Wednesday, 2/28—I called Gertie in Boston via Google Hangouts and came out to her. She was totally copacetic and a source of counsel and comfort.

- Thursday, 3/1—I individually msgd. the boys to arrange my visiting them, but each was so worried about what news I'd give that they insisted I tell them over the phone. Atti said he had no reaction but needed to process. Liam was not accepting at all. Later that day, he contacted Pam.

Friday, 3/2—Pam came home, and we talked. She continues to process. We came up with the idea of renting the next-door apartment that's opening up so that I could go there any time I want to be *en femme*.

- Saturday, 3/3—Liam called Pam and told her that he doesn't want me around him or his family *en femme*, and that he, Sharon, and Elanor wouldn't be visiting soon. He also related a phone conversation he'd had with Atti, and Liam's account of it seemed, again, to reflect more of his anxiety than that of Atti.

    I'd had enough of his speculating with others about my situation instead of talking with me. I wrote a long email to Liam. I've yet to hear a response.

Liam,

If you have concerns about me, I'm the person you need to go to with them. That being said, I can anticipate those concerns:

Concern (1): *Are you nuts?*

The potential of being insane is something I've lived with and not let even those closest to me know about for my entire existence. What seems out-of-the-blue to you has been with me all my life. Because you're grieving this, it's a crisis you want to nail down with some explanation. I understand that 'cuz I, too, my whole life, have been trying to explain myself to me.

Concern (2): *How can you do this to Mom?*

Mom is a formidable counsel and caution, even while she agonizes over this. I face the hurt she's going through, as well as the possibility that I'll lose her. But I won't be a better spouse to Mom by lying about who I am.

We spend many nights talking, crying, snuggling—in short, dealing with this grief. For it is a grieving. What I thought myself to be never was! I'm grieving that. Some of Mom's empty-nest expectations of our relationship are also gone—but they would've been gone whether I'd come out or not. I was never going to be the husband she expected, nor could my sham at being one have fulfilled her expectations, even if I'd decided to repress this truth about myself. In fact, things would be worse, as I would be lying to her—not just about who I am, but, worse, about why I was a moody asshole who lashes out in anger.

But it's not just a one-way street. Your Mom has her own way of telling me/not telling me things. She, too, in this marriage, has had her not-so-even-keel moments. But she and I have always tried to craft an environment in which the two of us can wrestle with these things … and be who the Beloved makes us to be. Give us the space to figure this out ourselves.

Concern (3): *Isn't this a reckless decision, similar to the reckless decisions your own father and mother made, and which you rose above?*

I didn't wake up one day and say, "I am a woman," and suddenly become what I thought to be a woman. That's not what being trans is about. It's an awareness that who and what I am does not mesh with the societal expression of the gender binary.

My father and mother could not rise above differences they brought into the marriage. Could they have proceeded differently from the beginning? Yes, and I've arm-chair quarterbacked the breakdown of their marriage ever since. They acted in ways your Mom and I have resolutely not.

"But," you might object, "Even if this trans thing is an 'awareness,' you don't have to act on that awareness, like your parents did in divorcing."

Liam, you became aware, at a young age, that you wanted to pursue bass guitar. Mom and I waited to see if it was a passing thing. But it wasn't. And, true, you might not have been allowed to act on it because of, say, financial constraints that would've prevented us from financing a bass and lessons. But you did act upon the awareness. We were blessed to have you become a helluva a musician and composer. Of course, you didn't have to act on it. But you wouldn't be who you are had you not. In other words, you wouldn't have been true to you.

It's a clumsy analogy, of course, for gender awareness is different than a thirst for a musical vocation. Or is it? Both are expressions of the self, and we all struggle with ourselves and the world to become the truest version of ourselves that we can be—i.e., we learn it and, if we have the chance, we make it real.

"But," you might also object, "There's a more significant difference between trans awareness and wanting to be a musician: one is wrong and the other is value-neutral."

And that's ultimately where we differ: you believe my transgender awareness to be intrinsically wrong. I believe it is intrinsically right—it is true not only to the person I know myself to be but to what the Beloved calls me to be. If I stifle that, will I save Mom and my children anguish and alarm? Will I save my friends and loved ones a lot of cognitive dissonance? Will I stop from challenging the current societal constructs of the gender binary and stop causing a fuss to other people? Possibly.

But at what price? I will:

- be untrue to your Mom, lying to her each and every moment of every day.

- be untrue to you and to my grandchildren, lying to you each and every moment.

- be untrue to all my friends and loved ones, lying to them with my very presence.

- fail to challenge the prejudice and violence of a culture bent on enforcing a rigid, tyrannical view of gender, one that is limited to a very rarefied culture and time period.

- lie to myself.

Concern (4): *Aren't you risking your mental health, your job, your standing in your community, and your chances of suicide/violence?*

I've pointed out earlier that this transformation has been a blessing to, and healing of, my mental-health issues, because those issues were themselves symptoms of latent gender dysphoria. I'm also under professional mental health care. My workplace is LGBTQIA+ friendly, and I have a solid standing with the company. Further, I am armed with all the necessary legal procedures pertaining to coming out to one's employer.

My standing in the community is fine. Sure, there are folks downtown and at Rev who are scratching their heads, but I've received nothing but support and affirmation—something in very short supply from those communities that call themselves followers of Jesus.

The trans suicide and murder rates are so high (especially for trans teens and trans people of color) because of discrimination, transphobia, and a gender-binary-obsessed society that forces many (who don't enjoy the means and resources I do) to fall to hopelessness or murderous hatred. What's more, gender dysphoria affects people differently, with some experiencing it more severely than others. I'm in a good place. I never in my life, with all my mental and familial difficulties, ever had to contemplate suicide. My coming out as trans has brought healing that further precludes suicide.

Concern (5): *What exactly does it mean for you, Dad, to be transgender? How does this play out in real life?*

1. I'm not yet certain on undergoing HRT and/or surgery. That's why I'm seeing a therapist, starting in a therapy group, and meeting with a support group. If I in the future feel the way I do right now, I would do HRT in a heartbeat. But I want to examine this under professional care and the counsel of friends and loved ones.

2. I am transgender. That's a fact, Jack. I am so happy and comfortable as female. I have never been happier. Whether I get HRT and/or GCS, I am already transgender. I am who I am.

Concern (6): *What happens if you do take hormones and get surgery?*

- HRT eases gender dysphoria and is thus a treatment of the mental condition accompanying being transgender in a gender-binary society. It will treat my underlying mental issues much in the same way it has for hundreds of thousands of trans persons who have undergone it.

- HRT involves taking low dosages of estrogen which has the physical effect of shifting fat from the stomach to the hips, possibly reducing genital size, and enlarging the breasts, as well as reducing body hair and promoting growth of head hair. In addition, lessening of arm strength can also be a factor.

- HRT also involves taking testosterone blockers, so it can result, initially, in lower libido. But in the long term, that evens out.

I've no idea whether surgery will be for me until I profile 24/7 as a woman and undergo HRT. It may never be available/attainable for me anyway, due to cost and the simple fact that I'm 54. One thing at a time.

Concern (7): *I'm concerned about having you in my life and that of my family and children with you as transgender.*

You may feel that I'm anathema to what you believe and what I taught you growing up. I love you, and I know that you speak out of your love for my well-being and have to balance the needs of yourself, your family, and your beliefs. Thus, I will never hate you, even if you say you can never abide who I am.

I would be heartbroken if you cut me out of your life and that of Sharon's and Elanor's. But I know that's a price I might pay. If, however, you want true enquiry and dialogue, you know I'll always be here. I want to meet with you in person. But I'll go at the pace that y'all are willing to proceed, even if that means never. I'm still your Dad. Always will be. I love you.

∞ ∞ ∞

A lot can happen in a week. Looking at my entry for 2/24, I'd no clue that my coming out was upon me. I need to let Liam process things, and Pam to continue her own journey.

MORE HAS HAPPENED!

On Thursday, March 8, Pam and I went to Amico Nave for dinner. When we came home, we talked a long time and, sadly, agreed to separate, Pam taking Apartment 205 next door. I was horribly down and numb, but ready for the next step. If this was the way it had to be, I would continue down this path. I took an Ambien and went to bed.

While I fell asleep, Pam had a revelation that my confirmation as female didn't change anything about her love for me or about our 35 years of relationship. She said to herself, "Okay. I finally got resolution on the situation. So why is separation making me miserable? Bethany can be whoever she wants. I still love her."

She spooned me in bed, and told me that I could be who I wanted to be and that she was fine with it. That she loved me.

I stirred, and, under the influence of the Ambien, I said to her, "You know, I took Ambien, so, I realize I could be dreaming, but are you fuckin' with me on this?" She giggled, and everything has been incredibly different ever since.

- I came out publicly on Facebook, to alert all those folks who aren't my local peeps. I had 1,031 FB friends when I came out. Now, I have 1,039.

- I came out at work. They've been incredibly supportive and doing all they can to further my gender confirmation.

- Liam and Sharon cut us out of their lives. It's an aching sadness that Pam and I continue to grieve.

- I came out to Brian. He was thrown for a loop but has been supportive and loving about it.

- Atti visited for a weekend and totally embraced me. His words: "My biggest concern was that you'd be a different person. But you're you. You're Dad."

- Gertie visited from Boston, and we had a blast! She took

me to Target to shop makeup and the clearance racks.

- I've put into action my legal name change. I expect a court date sometime in May.

- Pam and I did the great clothes swap of 2018, and I made out like a bandit! (Wish I could say the same for Pam.)

- Others have given me makeup, purses, and more fabulous clothes! I now get regular brow-waxings, manicures, and pedicures. My breast forms look excellent, and I'm nearly a pro at doing my own makeup.

- I continue to see Cindy for therapy and to go to my group therapy in Austin, as well as my once-a-month local support group. All of these have been tremendous sources of healing, processing, and community.

- I've gotten the ball rolling on getting HRT. I have a full psych eval on 4/17, after which I've an appointment with a local trans-friendly endocrinologist.

There's so much else I can't recall right now, but I've been growing happier in a way that has little to do with merely feeling happy/euphoric. I feel like *ME* for the first time in my life. I'm learning tons about Bethany. The next few pages recount my FB coming out and the responses I got.

FB COMING OUT POST (March 10 at 9:46pm)—

Okay, Peeps! I'm coming out on FB, as I've already done so in the local community. This is for my friends and loved ones far away who do not yet know.

I'm transgender (MtF) and am in the process of confirming myself as female. Pam is 100% supportive.

I've made available an attached explanation of all the nuts and bolts behind this evolution in my life. Read it; it'll explain a lot.

I'll soon be changing my FB profile name to Bethany, and my pronouns are "she/her/hers."

Zane

I don't care what you call yourself, as long as I can call you "friend". Love you, ya big lug!

Beth

Bethany, I am so happy that you are taking the steps to truly be you. You have been on my mind. I look forward to continuing to be inspired by your wisdom. Thank you for sharing your journey with us. Sending you so much love.

Katherine

However you identify, you are still YOU. Rock on, Bethany!

Betty-Ann

Cheers to you Pam and Bethany … It's all about love. And you both are loved. No matter what.

Ashley

Cheers to you, Bethany! Much love coming your way.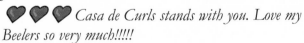

Devon

I am so happy for you, Bethany! Thank you for sharing your journey. Your strength continues to inspire me.

Jessica

 Casa de Curls stands with you. Love my Beelers so very much!!!!!

Dan

I'm gonna miss the beard. More power to you, Bethany.

Lisa

I never liked the long shaggy beard! LOL!

Codi

Way to go sister. BTW I have some size 10 heels and booties you may be interested in. XO

Chantal

You are amazing, Bethany!! XOXO 🪨

Savannah

Very brave and educational, thought provoking, inspiring explanation. Thank you for your courage. You are loved however you choose to be.

Xandi

So happy for you, Bethany!!! Thank you for sharing this.

Gregory

Very, very happy for you!! Sending my best.

Dana

I support you and am happy for you. I love you, Bethany and Aunt Pam. 🫶 ☺️

Jenna

I love you!!

Patty

I've always thought of you as an outstanding teacher and amazing person. I'm so happy you have an amazing supportive wife. Sending you all of the love and support!

Jill

Best of luck to you, Bethany. I admire your courage to become who you truly are, and I admire Pam for being understanding and supportive.

Shellie

Ok, so this is real. I am speechless.

Kerri

I'm so proud of you, Bethany. This takes courage and inner strength - thank you for demonstrating both and serving as a role model for young (and older) people struggling to find their space and identity.

Alan

Strength and serenity to you on your journey— may the road lead you to a better place, especially one with good beer.

Maggie

Julie

Congrats!! I'm so happy you have found out who you are!

Jamie

I do not judge someone by what I see on the outside and you are a wonderful person who I have known for a very, very long time. If this is something you feel you have to do, then I am behind you all the way. You are the only one who knows what is best for you. God bless you , Pam and your family

Bob [childhood best friend]

Promise me you won't post any bikini pics.

Susan

Bethany, you and Pam have had such a fascinating life journey. I learn so much from your openness to every twist and turn. Blessings as you continue to work toward being authentically you.

Amy

Congratulations on being your authentic, amazing self!

Laura

Be you, boo! Bethany is a beautiful name.

Maria

Bethany, thank you for sharing your story so eloquently. Sending love and support as you enter this new phase of your journey.

Stacy

Who knew that under all that beard was Bethany? Welcome to the outside world, sometimes it's cold and you may wish for the comfort and disguise of a beard, but being who you are is grand! I've always admired your love story with Pamalyn, and I can't wait to see what's next. Looking forward to more insights from your journey.

Clare

Love you Bethany. Here to give you support in any way you need. Thank you for being so open about your journey.
🖤🖤🖤🖤

Theo

I will roll one and smoke it in honor of Bethany and Pam and of active healing. Love you both!

Maura

L'chaim! L'chaim, Bethany. Bless you, bless you doubly, bless you infinitely for the courage you have summoned to be your authentic self. I know the taste of the freedom that comes from a declaration of personal identity. It is joyful and scary and everything else all rolled into one, now and moving forward. And the beauty of it is there is no going back. I wish you all happiness.

Cody

Congrats Bethany. Much love headed your way.

Kristin

Congrats Bethany! You're an amazing person, and so happy you have such a supportive loving family!

Sean

Love and Peace to you and your family!

Wayne

Much love to you, my friend! 👍

Cindy

🖤 *super proud of you & look forward to following your journey*

Julie

Like I told Pamalyn—you do you, my friend.

Cadence

Hooray for being courageous and living your authentic self! I also look forward to following your journey and good for you for going to therapy as you start your journey out.

Anh-Chi

Much love and admiration to you. Have a wonderful day, miss sassy Bethany!

Meg

Thank you for moving us all forward in coming into ourselves.

Clare

Life is hard enough without feeling like you have to be someone you aren't. I'm happy for you that you've found peace with your inner person. I'll send you and Pam well wishes in your journey.

Joe

I'm a little slow in reading this. I have tears in my eyes as I type. When life journeys touch me like that, I know I have been given a gift of something that runs deep. Thanks for sharing your coming out with Facebook friends. I love you Bethany.

Michelle

Be who you are. Be happy, joyous, and free.

Rebekah

Blessings my friend in this transition!

Jennifer shared your post.

Today I had the opportunity to read on FB one of the most beautiful things I've read in quite some time. One of my favorite teachers from high school revealed to the world who she really is. I can't imagine the strength and courage it took to take that first step forward, but I'm proud in a way that I can only compare to how a parent feels when their child does well, and the parent feel as if their heart could burst with joy. Welcome to the world, Bethany Beeler. You are smart, beautiful, courageous, and are loved from all over the globe. You are now whom you were always meant to be, and I'm thankful for the woman you are, as well as the person you've always been. Much love and good vibes will continue to be sent your way, especially as you continue on your current journey. For anyone on my FB going through something similar or feeling as if they have no one to talk to, know that I'm here for you and I support your decision.

Jimmy shared your post.

From a friend who recently came out as transgender, this document is a fantastic explanation of what it feels like to be transgender, and it mirrors many of my personal feelings about my gender identity. Well worth a read even if you don't know Bethany personally.

Chapter 16

Some Folks Are Never Happy

I seen ya around for a long, long time
I really remember you when you drank my wine
Why can't we be friends?
—War/"Why Can't We Be Friends?"

The support and love I've received during and since my transition have been overwhelmingly positive. Further, being a privileged white trans woman drastically reduces the chances for hate-speech and violence to be directed at me. Yet, people will be people and voice their negativity. This chapter is about those few instances and how Pam and I dealt with them. One was via social media. Another was from a former student of mine. Last, and saddest, Liam and Sharon cut us out of their lives.

Some folks'll never be happy. Their loss. 'Cuz I'm fabulous.

Negative Nellie

I saw only one negative comment posted, in response to a positive one a friend of mine, Melissa, had made. And guess who the Negative Nellie was? The mother who'd falsely accused me and Pam when we were teaching. Some people just keep on giving. Here's the original thread.

> *Melissa*
>
> *When I told our children and showed them your pictures, the older 3 responded with comments like "You have to be true to yourself," and "People just need to be happy and at peace." Youngest one, still a baby, said "I am so happy she shaved her beard, 'cuz that would have been awkward."*
>
> *Bethany Beeler*

O m'gosh! My heart is melting!

Clare

You raised some great kids Melissa.

Negative Nellie

Really? That is not what my *children said! Because they know God does not make mistakes. Does "he" have a penis? Then he is a man. PEROID!!* [sic]

Amy

Negative Nellie, you are being incredibly insulting and rude. Bethany is one of the kindest, wisest people I know, and she does not need or deserve your bullshit.

Bethany Beeler

Negative Nellie has always been full of poo beyond her eyebrows. I have no surprise that some of it is overflowing into her silly posts! #iamsofreeofheridiocy

Amy, you ROCK da Casbah … and MORE, Gurl!!

Gertrude [you guessed it—my bad-ass daughter]

Negative Nellie, you may think G-d doesn't make mistakes, but you sure did in the way you raised your children.

I'm assuming these are the same children I went to high school with who routinely cheated and plagiarized, who brought and consumed alcohol on school grounds and overnight trips, who physically assaulted other students because of the color of their skin, and who had pre-marital sex in a storage closet on Catholic school grounds.

Yah, probably best if you and your kids keep your close minded, bigoted, not-based-on-anything-religious opinions to yourselves.

Linda D.

Negative Nellie, you are absolutely correct in saying G-d does not make mistakes. G-d knew exactly what to do when giving Bethany the courage and strength to discover and to share her authentic self with the world.

Bethany Beeler

Linda D., have I mentioned lately that I love you? Well, if I haven't, I LOVE YOU! <3 <3 <3

Christopher

Negative Nellie, I really do feel sorry for you. To be trapped by so much hate and anger must be miserable. I too was once a judging asshole. And let me tell you this—once I released that part of myself, I found that I am so much happier . I'm going to pray for you, because your life must really suck that you have to tear down others, to make your own pathetic life appear better.

Zane

Ok gang, this comment thread is at like a 6 and at risk of fizzling out. I need it to be at least a 9. Negative Nellie, please reply back with some silly nonsense (you know, the whole "g-d this, g-d that" thing). Gertrude, you're the wrecking crew, so please remain on standby.

Melissa

My benign post about my children's reactions to Bethany and her journey started this insanity. Are we still in 8th grade? Cause that's how this feels. Comments made were an insult to me and how I have raised my children. Yet, I delight in knowing that I have raised honest, loving, tolerant, non-hypocritical children. Are my children without fault? Hell no. I love Bethany and Pamalyn Rose-Beeler for they have taught and cared for my children. If you have a problem with this or me ... Umm, I don't care.

Bethany Beeler

*Melissa, the proof is in the pudding; you and your spouse
are fine parents, and your kiddos show it. Negative Nellie's
is the reaction of tribe-keepers who hate themselves so much
in their own hearts that it rankles them when others free
themselves to be who they are. Silly asses.*

A Former Student Scarred By My Self-Hatred

Via Facebook Messenger:

FEB 12TH, 7:55AM

<u>ME</u>—Eric, if you are able and wouldn't be pained by it, I would meet with you.

<u>ERIC</u>—I can do that. We need to talk about all of this. I don't think I will ever be able to move on if we don't. I literally called into work just now because this makes me so sick. I can't keep doing this.

<u>ME</u>—Me, too. When are you free? We can meet at a place downtown. I need to face this, though it won't undo your pain or justify anything. Ain't here to defend myself. *Am* here to prevent us from triggering each other and to heal. 😞 😎

FEB 12TH, 9:31AM

<u>ERIC</u>—I went ahead and went into work, I'm here now. I'm willing to meet up with you but maybe not today.

<u>ME</u>—Good! I'm glad you were able to get to work. Let's look at a day later this week, when it won't impose on your schedule. You can pick the venue, or we can do it at my place. Your choice. Thank you.

FEB 27TH, 9:53AM

<u>ME</u>—Hey, Eric! We've really got to meet. I know that my very presence is a trigger, but there's important stuff I've got to tell you. Are you available in the next couple of days? I'm open 5-8pm. Where's convenient for you?

MAR 10TH, 9:42PM

<u>ME</u>—Eric, I've some news to tell you that will be a shocker, but I wanted you to know before you see it on FB. I've been trying to meet with you for a month now to tell you in person, but I assume your schedule hasn't allowed it.

I'm coming out on FB tonight, but I want you to know directly: I'm transgender and am in the process of confirming myself as female. I've made available an attached explanation of all the nuts and bolts behind this evolution in my life. Read it; it'll explain a lot.

I want you to know that *I DID NOT KNOW THIS ABOUT MYSELF WHEN I WAS TEACHING.* In fact, perhaps my then hideous beliefs were themselves a symptom of my latent status. I don't want this to be another trigger, but I also didn't want you to hear about it second-hand. Let me know if you need to meet with me or if you just hate my guts. Either way, brother, I will respect you and the space you need to keep.

Love—Bethany

MAR 11TH, 12:53AM

ERIC—If I could kick your ass right now I would.

All of this has been about you all along. You didn't feel bad for what you did. You just wanted to clear the air before you came out.

ME—No, it hasn't been about me, Eric. I had no idea my early posts were triggering you. You lashed out. I tried to meet with you to let you know *EVEN BEFORE I HAD LET ANYONE BUT PAM KNOW.* So you could be at peace. But you avoided any mtg. Dude, I get your anger, but when is your anger going to stop being about me? You're letting this define you, and it just isn't so. I've apologized in all the ways I know how. Sad thing is: the *ONLY* threat of violence I've received since I came out has been from you, another trans person. 😔

ERIC—Don't ever lump yourself in with me, ever.

ME—Eric, I'll always let you go at the pace you need. 'Cuz I didn't previously. I'd love to keep you as a friend, but that's for you to decide.

APR 6TH 7:40PM

ME—Okay, Eric. I've tried, repeatedly, to engage you in a healing face-to-face convo. Apparently, you're not able to do that. I respect that. But no more angry posts or msgs. from you until you have met me face-to-face. Only seems reasonable and right.

ERIC—Because I wouldn't interrupt my evening to talk to you, about you? Nothing you've done is fair, honestly, so I don't really care about what's fair at this point.

ME—You had the chance to talk, but you ran like you've done all the other times you had the chance to talk. T'aint bout me; YOU'RE the one who freaked and threatened violence. You're the one with the

anger. I've said I'm sorry countless times, and you're the one who
can't handle that. I wanted to afford you some peace; you apparently
want to nurse your angst. Life goes on, Eric. Bye.

Definitely *not* how I wanted that to end. But it does underline
the harm that my words caused, years beyond their utterance,
even after I'd discovered those words condemned and hurt not
only Eric but also my very self.

In previous years, both Pam and I had apologized to Eric, and
he accepted our apologies and re-established a friendship with us,
both in-person and on social media. Then Eric took umbrage that
many in the community were applauding my LGBTQIA+ articles
and social media posts. Understandably, he saw a hypocrisy
between what I'd taught and my public statements now, and he
thought I was fraudulently positioning myself as an LGBTQIA+
advocate. Because we'd previously reconciled, I'd no idea that my
posts and articles were now triggering him, but there I went not-
thinking again. Eric lashed out on social media to the point at
which I reached out to him on FB Messenger, which started the
above thread. And you saw how the rest went.

My capacity to cause pain isn't lost on me. None of my
presenting this here is intended to exonerate me or poo-poo
Eric's pain and difficult journey as a FtM trans person who
attended a conservative Catholic school that also happened to
have a bonehead teacher who spouted off things I was ignorant
of, even as I was trying to satisfy my own sad need to be part of
the uber-Catholic tribe. I used to dwell so exclusively on the hate
and pain inflicted on me by others that I ignored or tried to
justify the hate and pain I then passed onto others. We go back,
Jack, and do it again, repeating patterns of behavior, until
something grace-filled breaks in, to blast away that vicious cycle.

If you pull any lesson from this book, it's that all of us have
been scarred by others' bullying, judgment, and hate—poising
(and poisoning) us to inflict that hate on others … right when we
need to treat others with the love, kindness, and benefit-of-the-
doubt that we ourselves depend on. So, these days, I pause to shut
my yapper. I try to handle with care those I come across. Because
they don't cross my path by accident. My story alone ought to

show that.

Grieving One Who Hasn't Died

Liam's cutting us out of his life was like a sudden break-up—a bad dream from which we'd wake up once he came to his senses. I imagine he might've felt the same way about us. But he's persisted, despite our entreaties, to reject contact with us. Sometimes it feels worse than his having died. I grieve my son, who lives.

I've gone through (and still go through) the various stages of grieving his loss. I've been so angry at him. Then, nostalgia kicks in, and I remember the cross-country baseball-stadium road trip he and I took when he was eight. Or his coming with me on a mission trip to Uganda, where he charmed that entire nation. Pam and I still quip his signature catchphrases—like when I'd rage about some inconsequential bullshit, he'd say, "You mad, bro?"

It's sad that he has never seen me happy like I am now—no longer exploding over inconsequential bullshit. After he refused to meet me in-person, his exiling email came two weeks later, just as swiftly and unannounced as if he'd died in a tragic accident.

In her *Mary Magdalene Revealed*, Meggan Watterson says,

I know I will see my son again. I trust this. Even as everything is uncertain. I will see him again.

And then … I feel the awareness of what love really does. I feel the way love functions as a bridge. That in loving we can't ever be separate from those we love. Cor ad cor loquitur, which is Latin for "heart speaks to heart directly." I am only ever as far away from him as I allow myself to believe I am. I am only as far from him as I am from my own heart. I miss him. And instead of thinking this, I tell this to him directly. I remember that I am with him always, from within. I tell him how much I miss him and just how much I love him.

So I tell you this now, my beloved, beloved son. I love you. I will always love you. No difference of heart or mind will keep us from seeing each other again. I am with you wherever you go. I grieve what you grieve. And though I can't know right now the pain you feel, I offer you mine, as a way to bear the load.

Usque ad infinitem.

Chapter 17

The Trials of A Lesser Beren and Lúthien

Long was the way that fate them bore,
O'er stony mountains cold and grey,
Through halls of iron and darkling door,
And woods of nightshade morrowless.
—"The Song of Beren and Lúthien"/J.R.R. Tolkien

And then one day, a day we never knew would come, the cocoon begins to hatch.
Just enough to feel a ray of sunlight on our face. Just enough to breathe in the fresh air and
hear the new life calling. While the Hero's Journey ends in surrender, like Yin springing
from Yang and finding the passive in the active, the Feminine's Journey ends in action.
Yang springs from Yin, the active from the passive. And as the cocoon opens, so too does the
world. While returning may not be easy and our life still not perfectly sorted, we will make
our way with the strength of the matured Masculine by our side,
and the Feminine herself transformed.
Leyla Aylin/Midwives of the Soul

So it's me I see, I can do anything
I'm still the child
'Cos the only thing misplaced was direction
And I found direction
There is no childhood's end
I am your childhood friend, lead me on
—Fish/"Childhood's End?"

In his email cutting us from his life, Liam said this:

> it's clear that the transgenderism* hasn't rid you of your
> depression ... Just like Methodism, Catholicism, or anything else
> didn't rid you of your depression. And at some point in the near
> future, life will throw something jarring, terrible, or sad at you that
> will reignite the depression back up to its worst (just like it did when
> you were a faculty manager, or at school, or in the UMC). Your

---

*Terms like "transgenderism" or "transgender" (the latter, when used as a noun) are dead giveaways of transphobia. "Transgender/Trans" is an *adjective*; never a noun. To call someone "a gay" or "an LGBTQ" or "a Transgender" is an attempt to render persons into things—to control or wipe out the "disorder" they represent to you. That's your problem. Grow up and learn to deal with people who don't fit your tyrannical idea of what they should be.

decision to dress like a woman and take hormones isn't a change from your past tendency to radically embrace a new ideology, religion, lifestyle, or whatever you want to call it. No, instead, it's the exact same pattern of behavior.

Given my history, Liam was warranted in leveling this prophecy. To him, from his distance away from me, it would indeed seem like more of the same old thing. Believe me, in my discernment, I countless times asked myself if I was spinning my wheels again in a hopeless cycle. Liam was right about only one thing—a jarring, terrible thing happened in the following months. Not just one, but lots of 'em:

1. My youngest son and daughter-in-law cut off our relationship with them and our grandchildren.

2. Pam was diagnosed with Type II diabetes.

3. Our apartment building caught fire.

4. Our misanthropic landlord made our apartment living conditions unbearable.

5. For Pam's health, my safety, and a better life, we moved out-of-state in the span of two weeks.

6. The loss of Pam's job.

7. The totaling of one of our vehicles, which nearly killed us.

8. The loss of my job.

9. Staying a month in Madison, Wisconsin to undergo and recover from gender affirmation surgery.

If ever there were a test of whether I was repeating dysfunctional patterns of behavior and whether our marriage could last through my transition, this was a gauntlet akin to the labors of Beren and Lúthien Tinúviel (sans the procurement of a Silmaril and the loss of any appendages in the mouth of a gigantic evil wolf). Given that we passed through these trials without having to die and be reincarnated by the Valar, I think Tolkien would have been impressed enough by our ordeal that he might've put it into "The Lay of Pam and Babsie."

Being Shunned

We'd always been a close-knit nuclear family, especially because we were so far away from our kids' grandparents and extended family. Add to that our career transitions and our having stayed in one location no more than six years, and you have the recipe for a family that works hard to ensure the integrity of the relationships among mother, father, and children, about which Pam and I were always therefore intentional, communicative, and generative of an environment in which everyone's concerns and feelings could be heard and addressed.

We all relied on one another, complemented each other's talents and differences, and knew each other implicitly. Pam and I anticipated the kids' individuating into their own lives and characters. However, that individuation and our now-adult children's establishment of their own lives on their own terms shouldn't make a stranger of any one family member to the rest.

In the vacuum Liam's sayonara left, Atticus, Gertie, Kent, Pam, and I have achieved a closeness and mature adult-to-adult relationship that had been missing as our oldest two left the nest and forged their way into the world, Atticus conquering law school and establishing himself as a practicing attorney and Gertie going to school in London to gain a bachelor's in theatre and become a professional stage manager and director. Journeys like those change people; yet Atti's and Gertie's metamorphoses not only solidified them as people in their own right but as wonderfully integrated and individuated persons.

In Liam's case, launching into family life with Sharon began to introduce a difference between them and us that felt like a white noise background. I could ignore it under the clamor of interacting and visits, but I knew it was there when all was quiet. I felt like we were being watched and judged. Every life move we made that didn't mesh with what Liam and Sharon had in mind for us as grandparents became another chit on a list of grievances never verbally addressed. I wrote off my feelings as bogus, telling myself that they were young parents consumed with the work at hand. Anything but think that they could be watching us for a final straw that would necessitate their cutting us out of their lives. Not sure if that's how it went down in Liam's and Sharon's minds, but that's what their zero-tolerance declaration felt like.

The reasons for the separation seemed, to us, ludicrous and implacable. Surely time and growth would erode the otherness Liam and Sharon felt about us. Even though we weren't the same persons who'd raised Liam, people evolve. Meant-to-be relationships weather those changes. And that's what we were grieving—we never thought it possible that a lifetime relationship with our youngest son and his family could die.

My own story, and Liam's owning some of my genes, gives me hope for future reconciliation. Will he always identify with his current tribe? Or will he, like me, chafe at the limits they impose? Until that time, I'll take his prophecy of my doom and gloom, and raise his wager with this hope.

Pam's Health

Pam's grieving the loss of Liam didn't take the same path as mine. Her disbelief that our separation from our youngest could be permanent separation hung on. If that had been her only grief, she would have weathered it for sure. After all, this is polygraphin', two-shots-of-tequila-before-the-spring-concert Pam. But right about this time, a reorganization at work transferred her from a beloved supervisor, gave her a new boss who wasn't a good fit, and showed all the signs of an eventual downsizing of Pam's department and position.

In addition, Pam has for two decades suffered from idiopathic neuropathy in her feet and lower extremities. She had battled it into submission via meds. However, in the summer, her neuropathy returned with a vengeance. With that came disruptions in appetite, sudden and sporadic fatigue, and a host of aches and pains. Combine that with job woes and grieving the loss of Liam, and by autumn, we discovered she had Type II diabetes. Suddenly, the times in our marriage when I had depression and anxiety amidst the school investigation, or when I had my sudden loss of hearing teamed with vertigo that necessitated my taking short-term disability were now reversed. I was the caretaker, even as I watched my wife, who'd always been a steadfast pillar, slide downhill. If ever there were a time for me to fall back into anxiety, depression, and dysfunction in the face of trauma and crisis, it was now. But the prophecy didn't work that way. Not only did I *not* break down, but the fact that my transition had given me relief from those lifelong debilitations meant I was there for Pam in ways I hadn't previously been.

And we would need it, because the place was almost literally gonna come down around our ears.

We Didn't Start the Fire

Perfect time for our apartment building to catch fire. In the midst of Pam's throes with illness, one night at 3am, she awoke to our neighbor screaming in the hall, his apartment aflame. I didn't hear a damn thing because I was sleeping on my good ear and the bad one was deaf to all entreaties. Oh, yeah—and *our apartment building's smoke alarms were not functioning*. Forgot to mention that.

Pam ran into the hall, literally ripped the fire extinguisher out of the wall, tossed it to our neighbor, and called 911. The dispatcher, upon learning that our fire alarms weren't operative, immediately ordered Pam to clear the building. She didn't have time to get tequila, but, neuropathic feet, the diabeetus, and all, she tore up and down three flights of stairs and pounded on every door to summon all the residents before the police and fire team arrived. Oh, she also woke up me, who had slept through her heroics. Way to go, Babsie.

We then stood in the rain for the next hour as the fire department took care of things. The flooding caused by the sprinkler system missed our apartments by a couple of feet, but our neighbor's apartment and adjacent units were soggy, smoke-reeking crevices in Mordor's anus. The fun didn't stop there. This of course rattled Pam. I didn't freak 'cuz *I* hadn't been the one hollering and hauling ass up and down smoke-filled steps. I stepped in when the extracurriculars of the fire reared their ugly head (or ugly stench, as you'll see). So, again, a terrible jarring thing happened. Though Pam bore the scars, I didn't fall into old behaviors but said "Myeh" in the face of it. Sort of.

Which leads us to …

… Irreconcilable Differences with Slumlord Arms

Here's the thing about sprinkler systems. They're filled with water. *Duh*. Water that sits moldering in pipes for years on end. In the case of Slumlord Arms, that would've been *15 moldering years*. That shit doesn't smell good when it comes out of the pipes. Combine that odor with the smoke and fire damage done to the neighbor's kitchen by a rampant grease fire and the soaked foodstuffs of the aforementioned kitchen, along with a seared, non-functioning refrigerator full of perishables that had sat in an un-air-conditioned apartment in Texas autumn heat (it regularly stays in the 90s into November), and *Eureka!*—stench fest.

In their finite wisdom, Slumlord Arms (SA) saw fit, three weeks after the fire, to finally have the apartment cleared out. For this task, SA hired persons whose acumen made Moe, Larry, and Curly look like Hawking, Einstein, and Turing. On a fine Saturday morning, these three alumni of Dumb, Dumber, and Even Dumber University open wide that desecrated apartment door to clean the kitchen and refrigerator.

Mother of Severe Mercy.

The charnel odor crept under the doors of our two apartments, making us sense that something was rotten in Slumlordville. Then we heard scrambling and shouting and retching in the hallway. 'Twas then we made the mistake of opening our doors to see, What ho! was the happenstance.

One guy was projectile vomiting all over the hallway floor, the other two dragging him out while trying to hold back their puke and avoid getting slathered in his. All the while they left gaping the door to the source of this senses-raping effluent. Verily, we were not impressed. So much so that Pam started puking. I got her out of the building and called yon owner of Slumlord Arms who told me that my account of chaos at the establishment was verily full of shit. And hung up on me.

"Bob" This-Aggression-Shall-Not-Stand Beeler would've called the National Guard, the Coast Guard, HUD, the Chamber of Commerce, and the Boys and Girls Clubs of America to yell, holler, imprecate, masticate, castigate, and whatever else "Bob" could do to cajole, bully, reason, chide, curse, and travail the authorities as to this cosmic injustice.

Bethany just didn't pay the rent. We'd had a year-long list of repairs, bug problems, and fire-alarm issues that Slumlord Arms had ignored. So, Bethany let the lack of rent do the talking.

In the meantime, she proposed to the by now thoroughly shell-shocked Pam that they …

… Move to Colorado

We'd done a brief vacation late-June in Loveland, Colorado, about 50 miles north of Denver, and we loved it. The Rocky Mountains have been Pam's spirit animal since she was knee-high-to-an-eye.

I said to Pam the day of the Stench Trial, "Let's move to Colorado."

Pam picked Loveland.

The rest is history.

I don't recommend procuring an apartment, sight-unseen, in a location 850 miles away even while you're trying to move and get rid of two apartments worth of creaturely comforts and intending to skip rent with no forwarding address. Legally speaking, we were standing on firm footing, as refusal to pay rent is a verifiable recourse when all other ones have been denied. That being said, I did finally pay the rent to Sir Asshole, dropping it in the rent slot the night before we moved out. I did not, however, include any lease-breaking fees, as the Asshole would have to deal.

No muss. No fuss. No "Bob" explosions or anxiety.

In two weeks, we'd done it.

In Colorado, Pam healed—in part because

- Our new apartment is swank (and has operative fire alarm systems).

- She doesn't sweat at the blink of an eye (a hazard of living in the devil's ass-crack known as Texas).

- She can (and does) legally procure herbage that solves her neuropathy.

- She knows I'm much safer as a trans person in Colorado than in the hate-hole Lone Star State.

- She can camp in environs where cold-weather camping is not a wistful dream from which she wakes up in a puddle of Texas sweat.

Working remotely as we do has always meant that we can be anywhere there's internet access. So why not move to a place that's gorgeous, the people are laid-back, and you can have snow in the winter and less perspiration in the summer?

Yeah, About That Job Thing …

Okay, so Pam's finishing her disability leave when her workplace does the feared downsizing of her department. We're in Loveland for just three weeks, and Pam meets with her boss and HR to find she'll be out of a job by February 1.

Time to circle the wagons? Aw, hell no! You think this is "Bob" and shell-shocked Pam? No way. This is Bad-Ass Babsie and Back-in-Black Polygraphin' Pam!

Pam and I didn't freak. We didn't condemn the company as a bullshit tribe from which we had to divest ourselves. Actually, Pam landed one of the few open positions available and had a new, *higher-paying* job in the organization by first week of January.

I, however, began to explode … in terms of creativity. Since early 2019, I've, among other things,

- Written, done the voice-over for, and self-published three novels, with another one to be published in a few months.

- Painted 70 paintings, a number of which I've sold.

- Held an art show in Loveland.

- Launched my own website.

- Secured a Colorado therapist and medical team.

- Researched, decided upon, procured, and underwent gender affirmation surgery.

- Oh, yeah. I also wrote this memoir.

I haven't set foot in a church since coming to Colorado, and my body, heart, mind, and soul are better for it. Not saying that church should be outlawed. It works for some folks, but it ain't Pam's and Babsie's cup of tequi—uh, er—*tea*.

Lest you think it's all fun and games, and that I'm just tooting my own horn to discount Liam's prophecy … as Pam and I geared up to go to Madison, Wisconsin for my gender affirmation surgery and month-long recovery, June threw us two jarring, terrible, sad things that, again, we lived through, like most well-adjusted normal people do.

Hey, let's nearly get killed, then lose another job …

As we drove down I-25 to go to Denver's Pride Festival, we hydroplaned on a wet spot and did a hellish do-si-do across two lanes of traffic and spin-o-rama-ed fifteen times into the median (which, though it totaled our car, thankfully kept us from gliding at 50 mph into oncoming traffic). When we came to a halt with nothing worse than a seatbelt burn on my person, I saw that my floral-pattern wedges were still on and my pink cocktail dress was in place. Then the car door opens to, I kid you not, a Valkyrie-gorgeous female state trooper with the most stunning eyes. I knew then we would be just fine.

Two weeks later and four days before we flew to Wisconsin for my surgery, our company did a bigger downsizing, cutting one-third of its workforce, including Full-Time Faculty, effective November 1. However, my severance package was so generous that I'd no pressure to immediately get another job.

I knew we would be just fine when Pam and I agreed to a Lebowski-/Dude-inspired action plan to counter this cosmic aggression: "Screw the details of the severance and their cutting my job after 13 years. The number-one goal is to see through this surgery to full recovery."

Correction: I knew we'd be just fine because *who needs a tribe when you've got each other?*

Pam and I, looking ADORBS!

Babsie, post-surgery. All the pumpkin-heads adore her!!

My future[and PRESENT]'s so bright, I don't give shade, I wear shades!

Chapter 18

This Is How It Feels: A Trans Finale

Take a little trip back with father Tiresias,
Listen to the old one speak of all he has lived through.
I have crossed between the poles, for me there's no mystery.
Once a man, like the sea I raged,
Once a woman, like the earth I gave.
But there is in fact more earth than sea.
"The Cinema Show"—Peter Gabriel/Genesis

We will wear your white feather
[All the children]
We will carry your white flag
We will swear we have no nations
[Beirut children]
But we're proud to own our hearts
[Jerusalem children]
We will wear your white feather
[Tokyo children]
We will carry your white flag
[Moscow children]
We will swear we have no nations
[Washington children]
But we're proud to own our hearts
[Munich children]
These are our hearts
[Chicago children]
These are our hearts
[Cairo children]
You can't take away our hearts...
You can't steal our hearts away
I can't walk away, I can't walk away
No more, no more, no more, no more …
—Fish/"White Feather"

I'm not gonna tell you what it means to be transgender. Nor what it means to be female. I know far too little about either subject, and I'll be learning them the rest of my life and beyond.

I'm just gonna tell you how I feel.

Since my public coming out, peoples' responses have been astonishingly compassionate—especially that of my amazing wife, Pam. The loving reception I've enjoyed is matched by how it feels to love myself after a lifetime of doing anything but that.

In the beginning, words for LGBTQIA+ persons were "fag," "dyke," "trannie," "pervert," and, sadly, more. We didn't have our own words because we weren't permitted to speak, weren't allowed to feel. When we did speak among ourselves, we more likely than not used those slurs for each other, even as the troglodytes were burning the nightclub down around us.*

People weren't more decent then, and they aren't more decent now. People are people, in any time and place. What's different is that we're now the tellers of our stories, the feelers of our feelings. Back then, the only words and feelings we had were the slurs. Today, they'd have it that way again, if it hadn't been for a crowd of "trannies" in Compton's Cafeteria who found words to speak their riotous feelings, or a "dyke" who, being brutalized by police, incited a crowd to a riot of feelings outside the Stonewall Inn, the only seedy bar we were allowed to have. Then it extrapolated, as decades of LGBTQIA+ storytellers hollered *our* words for *our* deeply felt stories.

Those words became loud enough for even the densest folks like me to see that those stories were *mine* as well.

It's too late to shut us up. Once uttered, the feeling can't be taken back. The attitude encapsulated by the old slurs and tyranny was so engrained in the culture that my family of origin operated with "penis = male" and "male > female" as the implicit mode of being, imposed without feeling. It was the smog we breathed …

---

*They literally did burn the nightclub down in 1973. It was called The Upstairs Lounge, in New Orleans. This act of terrorism that killed 32 innocent people still remains unsolved.

... and it choked me for a lifetime, despite my most intense efforts to call that smog my life's breath. Being me became the labor of overwhelming people with smarts and over-meeting expectations so that others couldn't criticize, hate, or abandon me ... or see the real me within. I did such a bang-up job of it, that I had no real feeling for myself.

I felt around for tribes, jobs, churches, and communities that delineated who was in and who was out, all with the promise that, once I was "in," I'd feel out the true path. I proclaimed in pulpits, classrooms, and social media unfeeling hate in the name of sincerely-felt righteousness. Oh, I out-holied them, while crucifying myself on the splintery wood of an inner dilemma so lost upon me I never felt the nails driven in.

But I did have *some* feelings—never-relenting displacement, fear, and anger that inevitably led to my calling bullshit on tribes and being tarred and feathered.

This memoir doesn't nail a moment of clarity, when I realized it all. I can't call it even a dawning awareness because that implies I did it on my own. Awareness came via love, most manifestly embodied by Pam. Of course, she isn't the only love in the cosmos. But she's a damn sparkly lighthouse of it.

Gradually, like Eustace in C. S. Lewis' *Voyage of the Dawn Treader*, the Beloved scraped away dragon armor till I felt Her silver-crystal claws sink in. At the first puncture into the quick, I felt like I was going to die, shuddering and weeping, *"I love you so much. I love you so much!"* to Her. When my pain was answered by the shedding of scales, She showed me that I was taking the daring step of loving myself ... *as* myself. Astonished, I glimpsed the raw, pink flesh there, and I saw ... Bethany.

Dayum!! I didn't know what to think, which was just as well. I'd done way too much thinking. It was a sincerely felt riot of feeling. Bethany feels glorious! I'm me, in a way that I've never been. I like me. Hell, I *love* me! Without apology. Without fear. Without having to belong. 'Cuz I already do. To *me*.

The Beloved smiles back to me from the reflection in my still-teary irises.

Anticlimactic, huh? O, Reader, you were expecting that road-to-Damascus moment when the heavens opened, and the scales fell from my eyes? Shit, it's still happening. And will be. For the rest of my life. And beyond. *Usque ad infinitem.*

And it's glorious.

You see, in the end, and, in the beginning, trans people don't need a narrative of struggle in order to be trans. Sure, some of us have struggled. Some from their first childhood conscious awareness. Bully for them. Others not until they're 54. Bully for us! Still others are being loved, supported, and mentored by parents in a day and age in which the smog of self-hatred is being blasted away, no struggle necessary. Bully for everybody! Whether we're trans or LGBQIA+; Catholic or Methodist; John Bircher or Nudist Buddhist—we don't need a history, a struggle, or tribe to be ourselves.

I'm just learning that …

… my story is as unique as I am.

… the things about myself that are the most unique, the most different, actually land me in the human tribe.

… it isn't a tribe at all. No one's in. No one's out. We *are.*

… the better we tell our unique stories, the better we feel about ourselves and about each other.

Those that won't feel? Not our job to make 'em feel. If my story, my words, my fan-fucking-tastically fabulous presence can twinge 'em, that's nice. But I don't need 'em to feel in order for me to feel incredible about myself.

For me, *Once a man, like the sea, I raged. Once a woman, like the earth, I gave. Ah, but there is, in fact, more earth than sea.*

I'm feeling out this earth called "me." Feel free to join me. I don't know where it will take us. But I'm not afraid.

And the moral of the story is:

   I feel good. I knew that I would. Peace out.

Appendix I

You Want to Support Trans Folk?
Some Do's & Don'ts

I can pare down every cisgender (cis*) person's objection to/hesitation at my trans identity to this core whine:

> *"Your transition is a struggle for me and my culture. Rewriting how I once knew you impairs my formative memories/traditions. It's toxic to me to revise my memory and expectation of you. Your transition menaces my personal and our society's identity."*

Trans persons aren't asking cis folk to wipe your memory banks. I don't expect anyone to not remember my beard. I want you to be faithful to your memory. Yet, my being faithful to me demands your faithfulness to *who I am right now*. Say you and I are work peers, and I get promoted to supervisor. We might harken to having been workmates, but the new paradigm shakes that cohesion. It's not just you who has to adjust; I have to, as well—with everyone, including me—and must do so in a world that sees trans folk as exceptions expected to do 100% of the adjusting. I am commanded to defer to how others once knew me—under the rubric that I'm the one who's upending "normalcy"—when, like anyone else, *I'm just being me*.

Not only will I *not* conform to discomfited cis-het folks' gaslit rules of engagement, I won't come even half-way. The entirety of my pre-transition life I went *all* the way to be someone I wasn't so that your lot wouldn't reject, hate, kill me. Boohoo for cis folk. Your cherished memory of us and the world before we came out has to die to give way to new life. Yours won't cease to be memories. Accepting that they *are* memories is *your* job.

You have to do what all persons must—accept that the past is indeed *past*.

---

* Some cis folk protest that the term "cis" is a slur used to defame them. Hardly. "Cisgender" is derived from the classical-Greek root, *cis-*, meaning "the same side as" (i.e., your gender identity happens to align with your body's presentation—e.g., you live as an embodied male/female and experience your gender on the same side as your bodily presentation. The root, *trans,* means "on the other side of," indicating that our gender identity is *not* on the same side as/aligned with the anatomical presentation we were dealt. So, who's being ultra-sensitive? It's not trans folk, who endure denigrating epithets such as "trannie," "she-male," and other slurs. We us the roots, *cis* and *trans* to tell it like it is. Or is it really that you want us to call you "normals" and ourselves "freaks"?

Therein you might see the stunting your cis privilege has cost not only trans persons but you and the world. Your comfy past does not determine who you and I are now nor where we go next. Be *present* to me—*not* to your memories of me. You and I are more substantial and worthy of each other's attention, compassion, and respect than the past you can't get over.

Maybe you don't do this for trans folk because you've never dared do it for yourself. Stop demanding that trans persons pay the price of who you were, who you are, and who you're becoming.

To that end … you may have just discovered that an associate/friend/loved one is <u>*transgender*</u>*. Here are do's and don'ts to help you do the above and affirm trans folks' worth and dignity as human beings:*

DO Understand What It Means to Transition

Not all trans persons have the Caitlyn Jenner narrative (i.e., having always known they weren't their <u>assigned gender</u>). *Nor do they need any specific narrative to be trans.* We all have different stories.

DON'T Confuse Gender with Sexuality

I am, always have been, and always will be attracted to women. Other trans persons may be attracted to the same or opposite sex or be bisexual or asexual. *Vive le difference!* Think of the distinction between sexuality and gender this way: *Sexuality is who you get in relationship* with*; gender is who you get into relationship* as. So, that makes me lesbian. Confused? Don't worry about it. We love whom we love.

DON'T Assume That Being Trans Destroys A Marriage

Pam and I are lockstep on this. I owe everything to her courage, open-heartedness, and steadfast love. Unfortunately, though, many trans persons' confirmations lead to the dissolution of relationships and other family ties. I'm under no delusions that mine has been anything but a privileged ride. Thank God for Pam (and for my daughter, son-in-law, and son, who've supported me from the get-go)!

DON'T Assume A Trans Person Endangers Themselves

- My gender confirmation *healed* my life-long depression and anxiety, which illnesses were themselves symptoms of latent <u>gender</u>

dysphoria.

- My workplace (as are numerous others) is LGBTQIA+-friendly, and I have a long-standing relationship with the company. This is not the first time my organization has been part of one of its employee's confirmations. Sadly, a distressing number of Trans folk are discriminated against in the workplace. Their courage and conviction in gender confirming despite losing their livelihood is truly inspiring.

- I've received nothing but support and affirmation from my local community. That said, for the first 12 months of my gender confirmation, I lived in Texas. Although no one openly harassed me, given the trans-toxic culture of conservative places like the Lone Star State, I found existence there to be wearing. Since then, Pam and I (for many reasons more than just my confirmation) have moved to Colorado, which affords a safer and healthier environment. Not all trans persons have the means to escape their current toxic job/living/family situation. Still others choose to persist in a trans-antagonistic culture. I respect those situations and choices and wish nothing but fullness of life and love to all. I also do whatever I can to support them through their journeys.

- The trans murder and suicide rate is high because of discrimination, transphobia, and a gender-binary-focused society that destroys many trans people (especially trans persons of color). I've never contemplated suicide but completely understand why others do. The pain that leads to suicide is torture. Suicide is *not* a stigma or moral flaw; it's a consequence of depression and anxiety. The sooner we acknowledge that much depression/anxiety is induced by hatred and discriminatory public policy, the better we'll respond to those who feel their only recourse is self-harm.

DO Understand What It Means to Be Transgender

My confirmation as female is not a "switch" but is who I always have been. I'm transgender (MtF): my assigned gender at birth was "male," but I am a woman. Being trans is not about my waking up one day to present as female. Wearing feminine clothing, jewelry, or makeup isn't what it means to be a woman. It doesn't mean I believe that all women must be that way nor that all trans women *are* that way. Again, *vive le différence!* All women should have the freedom to be who they are. That our civilization abuses, subjugates, and demeans women is a hideous reality that we, hopefully (if glacially slowly), are turning around. My feminine presentation is not a masquerade or an attempt to discount feminism or women who present differently; it's one with my identity. #MeJustBeingMe, #YouDoYou

DON'T Ask Questions Like "So, have you had surgery?"

Asking trans persons about their bodies, sexual orientation, medical procedures, *etc.* is NOT supportive but intrusive, rude, and an assault on our human dignity. Would you ask a pregnant person what sexual position they used to conceive? Whether the pregnancy was wanted? Would you question the legitimacy of their conception if it were *in vitro?* Or ask what they'd do if their child has *in utero* complications?

Even if you feel like your relationship with a trans person allows such questions, ASK FIRST whether they're comfortable addressing such private matters. Don't take them, or your relationship, for granted; give *them* the agency to tell *their* story *their* way, in *their* own time, *even if that means they DON'T tell it to you.*

My story? (And I offer this openly; feel free to send me questions; there, see? I just gave *you* agency!): I'm on hormone replacement therapy (HRT) and have had gender confirmation surgery (GCS). Regardless of surgery or HRT, I have always been a woman. Not all trans folk elect to have HRT or GCS, *and that makes them no less than the gender they are.* "Male" ≠ "penis" and "Female" ≠ "Vagina."

DO Treat People with Decency, Love, and Compassion

If the above seems like Courtesy 101, then, you were brought up right. Sadly, until the world renounces fear and hatred, such compassion isn't a given. You haven't walked in our shoes, so love us as you want to be loved—especially in breaking the bread of words. To use Thumper's mom's advice: If you can't say sumthin' nice, don't say nuthin' at all.

Here's a quick itinerary to lovingly navigate potential flashpoints.

Pronouns—Some folks have "my pronouns" in their email signatures, bios, etc., to clarify their gender identities and empower trans people. My pronouns are "She/Her/Hers." Pronouns are as significant for trans persons as they are for cis folk. This isn't "special treatment" or "political correctness." How might *you* feel as a cis male if someone continually referred to you as "she/her/hers"? You'd think your interlocutor either utterly oblivious or picking a fight. *#WhenInDoubtAskAbout*

A Dead-Name/Pronoun At Any Other Time … Is Still Stinky Dead—I used a male dead-name/pronouns previously, but I've always been female. *How* you knew me then or know me now does *NOT* define me. Get our permission first as to the loving way to refer to us, past or present. If you don't know our pronouns and we aren't present to be asked our pronouns, default to "they/them/theirs" until you know better.

"Trans" Is An Adjective, Not A Noun—"Transgender/Trans" is an *adjective*; never a noun. To call someone a "gay" or an "LGBTQIA+" or a "Transgender" is dehumanizing—making them a "thing" instead of recognizing them as persons. We are *first* human beings. Some of us are American, Italian, or Coloradan; doesn't make us less than *homo sapiens*—just helps us locate nationality/citizenship/residency (i.e., how we identify).

Your Kampf—Just because *you* are struggling doesn't entitle you to an explanation—no matter how close you are to us. If we're close to you, we already know you're struggling. Why? *We've* been struggling with our true selves *for years, if not decades.*

Not Up for Discussion—You also don't have the privilege to "think out loud" with trans persons about our personhood, presentation, identity, or anything else you have the luxury of taking for granted as a private matter. Trans persons are NOT your chance to engage in trans-related philosophical, theological, ethical, or biological conjectures. If we initiate that discussion, go for it.

Take Us As We Are—WHAT YOU *SHOULD* DO when you meet a trans person or discover that someone you know or love is trans is to TAKE US AS WE ARE. By coming out as non-binary, genderfluid, gender non-specific, trans man, trans woman, or any other self-identification, we are *NOT ASKING YOUR PERMISSION TO BE WHO WE ARE*, nor are we asking your encouragement, support, or comment, however urgently you want to say something. We are *PEOPLE*. Take us as we are. Like dating or making a new friend, start out with small talk, discover common interests, and see where the night and our lives together go. Because you're meeting the real us for the first time.

To Those Who Object to A Sinful "Lifestyle Choice"—Those who use "transgender" as a noun (or hateful terms like "transgenderism") are no different than those who use slurs like "trannie," "she-male," etc. (At least the slurrers are honest about their fear, hatred, and bigotry.) Choosing your own grammar/nomenclature to refer to others in an attempt to express your "ideology" or "religious belief" is either a self-delusion or a prevarication designed to hide your bigotry.

Ideology/religious belief don't justify saying "down" is "up"; calling a blue sky plaid; or labeling Jewish, Native American, enslaved, and LGBTQIA+ persons (to name a few) as not human persons "created equal and endowed by their creator with certain unalienable rights." It's your attempt to render persons into things you can manipulate to your ends. Calling someone what *you* want to call them, despite their presented identity and the revelation provided by centuries of human experience, is *your* attempt to control or wipe out the "disorder" they represent to *you*. That's *your* problem. Grow up and learn to deal with people not fitting *your* idea of what they should be. *A la* the Rolling Stones, "you can't always get what you want."

If You REALLY Are Honest About Treating Trans Persons with Compassion and Respect—If you're in earnest about not wanting to offend—and you *should* be because *you simply have NO IDEA of whether you're in the presence of a trans person* (and, really, can you morally justify using the n-word when you think no black person is around?)—always *ask a person who self-introduces as trans what their pronouns are*. Though I have a Master's in English and have been a professional writer and teacher for decades, I have no qualms using "they/them/their" in referring to *anybody,* singular or plural. It's the most compassionate and efficient way to proceed until someone requests different pronouns.

DO Know That Trans Persons Bear the Burden of Being Human— My confirmation may, to some, seem an attack on their core values. When others comment to me as such or unfriend me on social media or in-person, I try not to be offended or to retaliate. Despite the loss, I know there are too many blessings in life to allow shunning to darken my horizon. I'm sad when I'm sad, and I'm happy when I'm happy. Life, in most aspects, is usually a combination of sadness and happiness. I can embrace that by embracing others.

For more information on what it means to be transgender and workplace policies on equality and equal opportunity in the workplace, respectively, please go to: https://transequality.org/issues/resources/frequently-asked-questions-about-transgender-people

Appendix II

Essential Trans Resources

Books and Articles

Julia Serano, *Whipping Girl: A Transsexual Woman on Sexism and the Scapegoating of Femininity*, 2nd Edition—Simply the best book available on the science, ethics, and issues surrounding trans experience. Read this, and you'll have most every answer to transphobes and TERFs.

Amanda Jetté Knox, *Love Lives Here: A Story of Thriving In A Transgender Family*—Written by a passionate warrior for trans rights, this memoir recounts the coming out of Knox's trans daughter, then her spouse of 18 years. Knox's indefatigable spirit, verve, and wit are an amazing antidote to the depression that accompanies gender dysphoria.

Jennifer Finney Boylan, *She's Not There: A Life in Two Genders*—The most winsomely written memoir of transition you'll ever read. It helps that Boylan also happens to be an accomplished novelist.

Mia Violet, *Yes, You Are Trans Enough*—My favorite of coming-out memoirs because Violet pulls no punches in her self-assessment, as well as aptly notes the tremendous roadblocks to transition and healthcare in Great Britain.

Helen Boyd, *She's Not the Man I Married: My Life with a Transgender Husband*— *The* best resource for spouses of trans women. Period.

Amy Ellis Nutt, *Becoming Nicole: The inspiring story of transgender actor-activist Nicole Maines and her extraordinary family*—A sensitive recounting of the journey of Nicole Maines, assigned male at birth (AMAB), who, at the age of three announced to her bewildered parents that she was a girl.

Andrea James & Deanne Thornton (Editors), *Letters For My Sisters: Transitional Wisdom In Retrospect*—Heartfelt and lived-experience advice, comfort, and reflection that is essential reading for every trans woman.

Antoinette Cavitt, "When Your Spouse Comes Out As Transgender," https://medium.com/an-injustice/when-your-spouse-comes-out-transgender-9287208ce1e3 In this brief but power-packed article, Antoinette concisely and winsomely sums up the experience of a partner/spouse faced with their partner's coming out as trans. Essential reading for trans partners, trans persons coming out to a partner/spouse, and those who want to support those in relationships experiencing a coming out.

Websites—Legal Issues, Advocacy, Support, Allies, etc.

National Center for Transgender Equality (https://transequality.org/)— Your one stop for navigating name changes, legal rights and access to medical care, trans activism and advocacy, and more.

LGBTQIA+ Definitions (http://www.transstudent.org/definitions)—I've found no better glossary of trans/non-binary/gender-fluid terms.

GLAAD's Tips for Trans Allies (https://www.glaad.org/transgender/allies) —Few organizations are better than GLAAD for LGBTQIA+ rights and advocacy. This page (and others on GLAAD's site) is particularly helpful for trans persons and the allies we need to support us.

Websites—Resources and Science to Humble Transphobes & TERFs

The Transition Transmission (https://medium.com/the-transition-transmission)—Edited by the eloquent Kira Wertz (and where I publish my trans-related articles), the TT is an epicenter of cogent argument for trans rights and the trans experience.

Between the (Gender) Lines: the Science of Transgender Identity— http://sitn.hms.harvard.edu/flash/2016/gender-lines-science-transgender-identity/

The XX & XY Lie: Our Social Construction of a Sex and Gender Binary— https://medium.com/@QSE/the-xx-xy-lie-our-social-construction-of-a-sex-and-gender-binary-4eed1e60e615

Stop Using Phony Science to Justify Transphobia— https://blogs.scientificamerican.com/voices/stop-using-phony-science-to-justify-transphobia/?fbclid=IwAR1jCPGEtbSi8fnrfHrAacxBn5GDZGqbMJ1js9oWSOEaTB3tkrRqlyxHJb4

15 Experts Debunk Right-Wing Transgender Bathroom Myth— https://www.mediamatters.org/sexual-harassment-sexual-assault/15-experts-debunk-right-wing-transgender-bathroom-myth?fbclid=IwAR1rXF8tLT0mXasK86o4KKtlG_eALu3bARVOmoAvgxc8NfKowbw_lchmwxM

Anatomy Does Not Determine Gender, Experts Say—
https://www.nytimes.com/2018/10/22/health/transgender-trump-biology.html

Don't Mess With Kira: A master class in responding to 'alternative facts' and willful ignorance—https://medium.com/@martiesirois/dont-mess-with-kira-f924242ff156

Study Results On Brain Patterns of Trans Persons—
https://www.ncbi.nlm.nih.gov/pubmed/19341803
https://www.ncbi.nlm.nih.gov/pubmed/27255307
https://www.ncbi.nlm.nih.gov/pubmed/21467211

World Health Organization: Gender & Genetics—
https://www.who.int/genomics/gender/en/index1.html

Understanding Gender—https://www.genderspectrum.org/quick-links/understanding-gender/

Transgender Adolescent Suicide Behavior—
https://pediatrics.aappublications.org/content/142/4/e20174218?sso=1&sso_redirect_count=2&nfstatus=401&nftoken=00000000-0000-0000-0000-000000000000&nfstatusdescription=ERROR%3A%20No%20local%20token&nfstatus=401&nftoken=00000000-0000-0000-0000-000000000000&nfstatusdescription=ERROR%3a+No+local+token

Reduction in Mental Health Treatment Utilization Among Transgender Individuals After Gender-Affirming Surgeries—
https://ajp.psychiatryonline.org/doi/full/10.1176/appi.ajp.2019.19010080

About the Author

Bethany Beeler is a writer and artist (she did the cover painting). She lives in Colorado with her wife, Pamalyn, and three cats of disaster, Big'uns, Frank, and Possum. For more information on her paintings and novels, go to
http://bit.ly/bethanybeeler

Other works by Bethany A. Beeler

Maria (of the angels)

Mirrororrim

The Fire Golem

Yanter (coming Spring 2020)

The Smoking Inn, With A Special Welcome to Lesbians, Trans Women, and All Creatures (forthcoming)

Caerdwain (forthcoming)

The Engine of the Avenging Angels (forthcoming)

Lawrence & the League of Short-Order Cooks (forthcoming)

The Bishop Tripped (forthcoming)

The Gods of Rome (forthcoming)

Master of the Universe (forthcoming)

Made in the USA
Middletown, DE
31 January 2020

83923208R00111